UNEXPECTED EXPERIENCES BEYOND AUTISM

DR. JALELAH
ABDUL-RAHEEM

Edited by
Karen Sue Redlack

Copyright © 2024 Dr. Jalelah Abdul-Raheem

ISBN: 979-8-218-38749-5

All rights reserved. No part of this publication may be reproduced, distributed, or transmitted in any form or by any means, including photocopying, recording, or other electronic or mechanical methods, without the prior written permission of the author, except in the case of brief quotations embodied in critical reviews and certain other noncommercial uses permitted by copyright law.

Book cover design and interior layout provided by Self Publish Me, LLC Publishing Consulting and Book Design Services for Independent Authors, Oklahoma City Oklahoma. www.selfpublishme.com | email: info@selfpublishme.com

To my son.
I pray you have all the happiness, success, and joy you deserve as you embrace your unique gifts.

Table of Contents

Preface 6

Chapter 1: The Beginning 8

Chapter 2: What I Learned in the Beginning
and Resources Used 20

Chapter 3: Early Signs In Daycare and Pre-School 24

Chapter 4: What I Learned From the Early Signs
and Resources Used 41

Chapter 5: Early Stages Of Finding the Right Resources 48

Chapter 6: What I Learned and Resources Selected 65

Chapter 7: Homeschool and the Pandemic 71

Chapter 8: What I Learned with Homeschooling, Pandemic
and Resources Used 86

Chapter 9: The Escalation 92

Chapter 10: What I Learned About DeEscalation
and Resources Used 103

Chapter 11: Partial Hospitalization Program (PHP) 109

Chapter 12: What I Learned During PHP
and Resources Used 122

Chapter 13: Inpatient Admission 128

Chapter 14: What I Learned During Inpatient Admission
and Resources Used 139

Chapter 15: Transition to Public School 145

Chapter 16: What I Learned About the Transition
and Resources Used 153

Chapter 17: Present Time 158

Acknowledgements 165

Preface

    The discussion on what the journey looks like beyond the diagnosis of a mental health disorder can be very overwhelming. As a parent of a child diagnosed with autism, I have experienced so many things that I didn't imagine would be in my reality. Even if people have no experience with autism, per se, I hope my experiences will help those who do understand the unexpected things that arise along the journey. None of it has been easy to deal with. There are days where I don't know what to do or know what is going to happen next. I've tried explaining to people my perspective only to still be misunderstood or unheard. Sometimes I unrealistically expect others to be able to respond appropriately, even though they don't have any clue where I'm coming from or the capacity to understand my situation. As an African American woman, it's been my experience that it is a difficult thing to acknowledge the struggle we experience when it comes to behavioral or mental health issues. That lack of acknowledgment and stigma within the community only compounds the problem and makes people feel isolated during tough times. I have found that my son's (Mahalek) autism diagnosis is a contributing factor that exacerbates everything else such as bringing unhealed traumas to the surface or even causing more trauma. I want to share my experiences about things I've dealt with along the journey with Mahalek. For starters, autism is often accompanied by other conditions such as anxiety, depression, or even medical conditions that make navigating through the experience that much more complex.

When people see me, I am typically told I'm strong, independent, and resilient. As a well educated African American woman, I'm perceived as strong no matter what life throws at me. To say that this perception of me is frustrating is an understatement. Not only is it frustrating it is also unrealistic. We all have our struggles and need support to help get through them. What most people don't know about me is that although I look well put together, I've struggled with having the right people in my life and I didn't always have the greatest support when I've shown my authentic self. I am also a victim of abuse. I've always worked two to three jobs as an adult, even with my level of education, to which has been my response to being in survival mode for so long. So, the resilience that people see is a result of my constant need to survive to make a better life for myself. I worked hard to lay a foundation so when the day came for me to start a family my children wouldn't have to struggle as I did. When I had Mahalek I really thought I had prepared for everything and had put myself in a position to create a safe environment for him.

Chapter I: The Beginning

I was filled with joy when I discovered I was pregnant. It was a surreal moment. I was proud of myself for doing things the right way. So, I thought. My perception of the right way was getting married prior to having children within a peaceful household. I had come up in a two-parent household that was very chaotic. For a short period of time, my parents had home daycare with several unwed single mothers who struggled to care for their children. My mother made sure to communicate how hard it was for them to raise children alone at a young age. She wanted her children to go about things in a traditional sense when we were ready and prepared to start a family.

I was advised to complete a college education to put myself in a position to be independent and help support a family. I was very motivated to go to college and I was a first-generation college student. I was determined to complete my education and be financially stable before I thought about having kids. I was so focused on completing my education, and making a better life for myself, I didn't address some of my childhood traumas until I was forced to when I had Mahalek. As I was completing my education,

I didn't really think about what it would be like to start a family. I just wanted to be able to stand on my own in a peaceful environment. At that time, I was subconsciously running from my experiences of being in a chaotic household and wanted to create the opposite. My thoughts on having a child were to have one or two within a marriage later in life. At that time, I wasn't sure when that was going to be after I had spent all those years completing my education. I got married shortly after that and Mahalek came a few years later. Although I thought about having a child eventually, it still seemed sudden and something I didn't think would be a part of my story. Nevertheless, I embraced the fact that I was going to bring a life into the world.

What I didn't see coming were the struggles I had to overcome to get pregnant when that time came. I had been on birth control since a teenager due to my irregular cycles and when I stopped taking the birth control so did my menstrual cycles. I have seen many doctors over the years based on my long history of intense pain and prolonged bleeding. I was recommended to a nurse practitioner around that time who discovered I have Polycystic Ovarian Syndrome (PCOS) and that is what made it difficult for me to conceive. After waiting several months, to see if my body would restart itself, the doctors advised me to start fertility treatment. I remember working as a nurse at the Children's Hospital around that time and had heard my co-worker's horror stories about their infertility struggles. I wasn't a fan of starting fertility treatment because I just didn't want to go through that or be monitored so closely.

When I made the decision to go through with the treatment, I was as prepared as I thought I could be. I was on fertility treatment for a little over a year. I felt like I had every symptom imaginable, but the main ones I remember were mimicking pregnancy symptoms such as pain, fatigue, mood swings, as well as just feeling ill and worn out all the time. The medication prescribed to help me ovulate was painful and taxing. After taking each dose I had to get my blood drawn to see if I ovulated or not. The repeated notification that I did not ovulate was so disappointing. I just felt like I failed as a woman because my body wouldn't cooperate. On top of that, my body refused to start my menstrual cycle on its own so my hormones were all over the place. This was all in addition to the daily temperature checks, monitoring the window of ovulation, and the numerous negative pregnancy tests. Mentally, I was defeated and after a while I decided to stop the fertility treatment and accept the fact that I may not be able to have a child naturally. I was tired of the disappointment such as the notice from my doctor revealing I didn't ovulate, the numerous negative pregnancy tests, and the ongoing hormonal shifts with symptoms that made me feel like something other than myself. When I got to a place of acceptance that being a mother may not be in my future, I found out I was pregnant.

The day I found out I was pregnant I thought it was just another day of abnormal hormonal shifts. That entire week I went to work so exhausted I could barely focus on the road. I was working at the university and it took about an hour for me to commute one way. It didn't occur to me that the fatigue was that bad, especially after getting more than eight hours of sleep the night before. Then one day I had a meeting in a city about an hour and a half away. I decided to drive along while I struggled to keep my eyes open on the way there and back. This was typically a meeting I had commuted to with my co-workers. As I drove and fought through my exhaustion, I began to conclude that I was just overworked, and I needed to take some time off and recharge. I had decided to pursue my doctorate degree in nursing that semester and contributed my return to school as a part of the reason for my fatigue. I honestly was in a space where I was allowing my body to return to baseline and looked for every other reason to justify my symptoms.

After the meeting wrapped up that day, I remember driving home being a lot rougher than the commute to the meeting. I instantly debated on stopping to take a nap at a hotel room before making my way back home. Besides, I was typically so mentally fatigued from all the information discussed during those all-day meetings I was truly done in every way that day. The drive back home seemed like it took forever. I ended up watching the clock, which seemed to move in slow motion, because all I could think about was sleep. I remember hitting a few rough spots in the road that shuffled me around in my seat and the touch of the seatbelt on my chest was so painful. I really was a bit shocked because I had never experienced that level of soreness before. When I finally made it home, as much as I didn't want to, I went ahead and took a pregnancy test. I got so used to reporting my symptoms to the doctor in the process and then following up with them telling me to take a test. I just figured I would get it out of the way before I let them know how I was feeling. My intent was to take the test, just to say I did it, and lay down. I took the test and walked away assuming the same negative result would show up. When I returned to the bathroom, I saw two faint lines. I was in a bit of disbelief that the result was positive.

After I got over my initial phases of shock, I began to reflect on stories my mother told me about how her pregnancy went with me and how sick she was. In addition to those stories, I started thinking about the things I've heard previously about pregnancy such as girls making you sicker than boys or girls taking your pretty away. I was getting nervous about how my body would change and what to expect. As far as the symptoms I would experience, I didn't really know what to expect. I felt like it couldn't be much worse than the symptoms I had while taking those fertility medications and the years of severe pain from my menstrual cycles. The first few weeks or so after I found out I was pregnant, and it was verified at the doctor's office, I felt pretty good. When I made it to six weeks, everything changed suddenly. I remember sitting in my office at work having a discussion with a co-worker and immediately feeling nauseous. I still can't remember what was discussed at that time because as that sickness hit me, I began to look around for a trash can or where I could go to vomit. Little did I know that was the start of being sick most of my pregnancy.

My pregnancy seemed very rough at that time. I had morning sickness all afternoon and evening from that six week mark all the way until my due date. There were a few weeks during that time that symptoms eased, but then ultimately returned. By the time I was three months pregnant, I got a B6 injection to help ease the nausea. I was planning to go on a week-long trip and didn't want to be sick the entire time. The injection worked for about 24 hours and then quickly wore off. All I wanted to do was eat a good meal without feeling sick, but it didn't work out that way. In my second trimester, I spent one day in the hospital to get rehydrated. I tried everything I could to get the nausea to subside such as ginger and ondansetron (Zofran). Even though I had vomiting episodes, the nausea was the worst part. The constant feeling that something was in my throat and burning my esophagus daily was so terrible at the time. I was able to eat decently until about 10:00 AM and then that nausea would return. I tried a few times just to force myself to eat, especially when my doctors were concerned about my weight loss, but it ended in a vomiting episode every time. My indigestion was so bad. The smell of certain foods such as chicken or turkey sausage made me want to throw up or made the nausea worse. I felt like I had food in my throat, the entire time, waiting to come up every second.

As the pregnancy went on, I was so malnourished my doctors had me meet with a specialist in my last trimester and debated the fact of inducing me earlier than my due date. My doctors were not happy about the weight loss and became concerned about what nutrition my son was going to be able to get with his rapid growth prior to delivery. In addition to my referral to a specialist, I was instructed to follow up with physical therapy as well. My son loved to sit close to my back and would often press on my spinal column. I would randomly lose feeling in one of my legs when he got big enough to move around pressing on my spinal cord. I was grocery shopping one day, lost feeling in my right leg, and ended up catching myself on the shopping cart. I was a home health nurse at the time, and I would occasionally do this while seeing patients in their homes as well. When I reported this to my doctor she was concerned for my safety and immediately sent me to physical therapy. I followed up with the physical therapist, as instructed, to reset my back and keep it in alignment to avoid falling and injuring myself or my son.

I had an innate feeling that I was going to have a son. I had a dream one night that I was in the back seat of the car with a little boy lying next to me and my arms were wrapped around him as we were looking out of the car window. When I woke up, I just knew I was pregnant with a boy. About a month later it was revealed during my doctor's appointment that I was expecting a son. Even though I had a feeling I was pregnant with a boy, I was still surprised about the fact that I was so sick all the time since I'd heard it was easier to carry a boy. It made me realize that some of the things I heard may be common, but vary with each person. I was very eager to meet the son I've always wanted. I was terrified at the thought of having a girl. I didn't think that I would be able to fully meet her needs since I was such a low maintenance girl and in some ways a tomboy. Besides, I didn't really style my hair much or put it in very simple styles. When it came to make up, I was just not interested in looking like something other than myself. When I did experiments with makeup, not only was I clueless, but it broke my face out 99% of the time. These were just a few things that made me feel like raising a girl would be more difficult for me. After it was determined that I was having a boy, I began to prepare for his arrival and started working in the nursery. I became excited about things such as names and nursing furniture.

I remained consistent with my progress in my doctoral studies as I got closer to my due date. I started to get feedback from my classmates and other people in my life about how smart they thought Mahalek would be since I was going through a graduate program during my pregnancy. This made me more motivated to complete my education, knowing how much potential he had prior to his arrival. I also wanted to make sure I was fully present for him when that time came. At first, I didn't think that I would be able to raise a child while working on a degree, but I wanted him to be proud of me and know that I did it for him, so I stayed on the course. I knew that if I took a break while I was pregnant or when he arrived, I wouldn't go back. I didn't think much about how things would shift after his arrival, with my studies, until I reached the last trimester. I was told by my doctors there was a possibility of him arriving earlier due to his low estimated birth weight and my sickness.

I am typically a pretty proactive person so before I had Mahalek I prepared other things outside of my graduate studies to make it easier when I returned home. For example, I made large meals to freeze so food could be reheated for at least a week after my delivery. I wanted to make things as smooth and easy as possible. I was grateful to be financially able to buy the things necessary for Mahalek's arrival and to organize the nursery as planned. Sometimes, I got pushed back from others who thought I should wait on baby shower gifts and things of that nature. There wasn't anything wrong with others getting things for Mahalek. However, I worked so hard to get to the position I was in, I was proud of myself for being able to get what I needed for him. I was still very thankful for all the gifts received to get him started along his journey in the world. As these things came together I continued to work, despite my struggles with nausea and vomiting along with the occasional dips in my blood sugar that last trimester. As my delivery date approached, I was just as ready as Mahalek was to enter a new chapter and phase of life.

At this time, my due date was at the end of the semester, so I tried to wrap up all my assignments at least a few weeks earlier prior to the winter break. My efforts to get assignments turned in a few weeks earlier, just in case I delivered prior to the end of the semester, made me so much more exhausted those last few weeks. Even with wrapping up schoolwork towards the end of my pregnancy I was still working full time and sometimes stopping to throw up in the middle of the street between seeing patients. Ultimately, things lined up well and I had Mahalek after the last day of class. After I had Mahalek and went home I became anxious at the thought of what it would look like to go back to school after the winter break with it being only a few weeks after his delivery. Mahalek was on a night schedule, and I was trying my best to get him on a daytime schedule, which was exhausting. I was always tired and got to sleep here and there so I was uncertain how I would remain attentive during my live intensive sessions for 12 hours each day to start the semester. After I completed those three days of live intensives, I began to plan how I would keep up with the assignments, discussions, and readings. By this time, my instructors had changed my status to full-time, to help me complete my degree faster, based on my worries about having to stop the program with a new baby. This posed another set of challenges I had to work through when Mahalek made his debut in the world.

With all the other moving pieces in place, I was flooded with so many feelings such as joy, peace, happiness, and fear. Mahalek had immediately given me a new outlook on life. I am a very selfless person and I was willing to give that much more for

Mahalek. The natural ability to just be his mother was so instinctive and automatic I didn't even have to think about what to do. The love I felt from Mahalek helped me understand the meaning of unconditional love. The concept of true and unconditional love was something I had struggled with understanding and made me question past experiences. However, the fact that this little innocent human trusted me, no matter what to do right by him, and accepted me entirely as his mother was the most refreshing feeling. I held on to that feeling and the thought that he would make a huge impact in this world with the right guidance. I was committed to becoming a better person and staying the course with my education to provide the best life for him. I wanted him to avoid some of the struggles I have experienced which meant I needed to protect him by any means.

Mahalek was a calm and happy baby for the most part. When I was on maternity leave, he would squirm and make subtle noises when it was time to change his diaper or feed him. It was rare that he would cry for long periods of time, unless I was out of his sight, or he was in the car seat. He would only tolerate the car seat if he was facing me unstrapped or when a mirror was placed on the back seat for him to see my reflection when he was strapped in. I guess some things never change because he still gets irritable at times if I'm not around. The thing that soothed him was different sounds and music. Sometimes I would have him strapped to me in his carrier while I vacuumed the floor. I noticed he would fall asleep to the sound of the vacuum every time. The sound of the vacuum was very soothing to him. To this day, he is fascinated with vacuums and volunteers to vacuum every person's floor he can. In addition to the sound of the vacuum, he has remained interested in learning about how it operates along with the types. As for the other sounds that were soothing to him, which were mainly nature sounds, he relied on them to help him fall asleep and stay asleep. As he went into his toddler years, I continued to play relaxing music for him on YouTube every night to help him sleep on his own. I was just happy that he was easily soothed and content so I could get some rest when he did.

Mahalek had quite a few people who wanted to come see him after he was born. They took turns holding him and getting cuddles in. There were times people held him and he would cry endlessly just because he wanted to be back in my arms. At least that's what I thought was the case. He was breastfed so I thought he wanted to stay close to eat. I was under the impression that breastfeeding him had increased our bond and he just had to get used to others. However, when he continued to cry and squirm nonstop it made me wonder what else was going on. Sometimes, I got tired of him crying so much I just asked for him back so I could calm him down. After he returned to me, I couldn't help but feel that with all the visits from family and friends he was getting overstimulated. To this day I still couldn't explain how I knew, I just knew. I would pick him up, take him to his room and rock until we both fell asleep. I played the soothing sounds on the music box attached to his bassinette and sang lullabies to him.

I was on maternity leave for three months and the time came quickly for me to return to work. I worked for a home health agency during the weekend, in addition to other part-time teaching jobs, to remain flexible as I worked on my doctorate degree. My intent was to do this until he got to an age where daycare would be appropriate. Mahalek remained happy and easy going. I did my best to make sure his needs were met so he would trust me to take care of him appropriately. He was my motivation to keep pushing through. I graduated with my doctorate degree a few years later right after Mahalek's second birthday. The relief I felt from not having to study or write another paper is an understatement. I felt like I could finally live, focus on my family, and find a new path in life that didn't involve school or being in survival mode.

Chapter 2: What I Learned in the Beginning and Resources Used

What I Learned in the Beginning

Throughout Mahalek's first years few years of life, I learned that my body was capable of great things and there was a strength in me that was unexplainable. At the same time, I learned that there was another level of fatigue when it came to the unpredictable schedule of caring for a newborn. This taught me how to go with the flow so to speak by becoming more adaptable and resilient. I became more adaptable to Mahalek's needs based on his personality. I developed a new sense of resiliency with the determination to be my best self.

I maintained a very structured routine to juggle everything. Mahalek was on a schedule that helped me predict things in a sense so I could plan around his needs and still be productive. The structure made it easier to care for Mahalek and I realized he relied on it. When he was thrown out of his routine, he would become very irritable and hard to console. Often it took a few days just to get him back in a good flow. After a few times of being off schedule, I tried my best to avoid interruptions to ease the burden of having to get him adjusted back. This led to some struggles with family not understanding the need for his routine. Sometimes I was hard on myself and let their perceptions get to me. I felt like I was bad as a parent or even making the wrong decision as I managed things with Mahalek. I learned that Mahalek thrived from a structured routine, and he was his best self when it was maintained. With that, it helped me trust my judgment on how things are managed despite others' opinions.

Lastly, I learned that my early feelings of him being overstimulated in certain situations were valid, even if I was unsure of the source. When we would attend events or occasionally visit with family or friends, depending on the environment, noise, and amount of people, Mahalek's mood was affected. When I recognized which settings had upset him or made it harder to console him, we left the environment. Although it seemed odd to others and leaving the environments were often perceived as me being overprotective or unrealistic, I dismissed the negative reactions and remarks. I had to trust myself to do what was necessary for him no matter what anyone thought. I had an unexplainable feeling that reducing environmental stimuli was what he needed. As I removed him and placed him in a quieter or sometimes familiar environment, he began to calm down. I was very in tune with picking up on his cues. So going forward, not only did I remain structured, but I became more protective of the environmental stimuli and environments he was in.

Resources I Used to Get Through the Beginning

The biggest resources I used to get me through this time were maintaining a structured routine, a calm stable environment, and investing in myself physically. Maintaining a structured routine wasn't perceived as the greatest choice and sometimes was seen as being unrealistic. This became a common topic of concern which typically resulted in ruffling feathers with loved ones who were not fond of the idea or wanted to interrupt that routine to get time in with Mahalek. The structured routine included a time frame for afternoon naps, bath times, and feeding times. I took the advice I had been given and rested every chance I got during those nap times and sometimes enjoyed an unsupervised and uninterrupted shower. This routine was so essential for me to be able to progress when I was pursuing my doctorate degree and still be present for Mahalek. Since it worked so well and helped keep things balanced it continued.

Mahalek thrived in a stable and calm environment. There were times where the environment may not have been the most appropriate depending on the circumstance. However, having the intent to keep him as calm and reasonable as possible helped with his mood and regulation. Determining the environments we went into ahead of time became a common thing. I'm sure there were moments when I was a little more paranoid than I needed to be at that time. As he got older and I got more acclimated as a mother, I learned how to control what I could. At that time everything was so new to me, and he was so small, I left a little wiggle room. What helped me keep a calm environment was limiting the number of visitors and the amount of time they spent at our house. This also included learning when to remove him from an environment, before it became too much, so I wouldn't have such a hard time calming him down.

I began to work even harder on myself physically. I wanted to be able to keep up with him as a toddler and be able to physically sustain my busy load. My passion was jogging. I loved jogging prior to having Mahalek and it was my outlet. After my diagnosis with PCOS and low blood sugar episodes I didn't think jogging was something I could do. I was under the impression that it made my blood sugar levels more difficult to control. I ended up getting creative with exercises that would be effective. I decided to work with a trainer to build myself back up physically and a nutritionist to learn different ways of eating. It was time for a change and to learn something new. Physical activity has always been one of the top ways I dealt with stress. I wanted to make sure I kept that outlet to stay balanced.

When I reflect on things back then I'm still surprised at the things I was able to pick up on when it came to Mahalek. I find comfort in knowing that even though I didn't know what the underlying cause was, regarding Mahaleks' behaviors, I was still able to be receptive to his needs. This made me pay more attention to him and trust my instincts. My intent was never to keep him from others, isolate him, or have him function like a robot, although sometimes it may have been perceived that way. My only intent was to keep him safe and make sure his needs were met. Little did I know that I was picking up on cues that indicated there was something much bigger.

Chapter 3: Early Signs In Daycare and Pre-School

The toddler years were a very pivotal time for me. Mahalek was introduced to daycare. It didn't set well with me for Mahalek to go to daycare with strangers and I was worried that he may not be treated appropriately. On top of that, I was so attached I didn't want him to feel that I was abandoning him and bonding with someone else because I had to work. The idea of staying home with him and at least working part time was what I really wanted to do. However, based on our situation it was not an option. Although I had an established career and enjoyed being able to make a decent living, I really wanted to spend every second I could with Mahalek and watch him grow up without the barrier of my job. I didn't always envision myself being a stay-at-home mom or slowing down for a child prior to Mahalek. He changed my whole outlook on life and my mindset after he was born. I struggled with the idea of leaving him to go to work, but I was thankful to be able to afford childcare.

Growing up, I was always determined to provide a better life for my family and was told having an education and career was the best way to do that. As a first-generation college student, I didn't have much direction or guidance into what that would look like or how to get there. My thoughts were if I obtained a college education and got married, I would be putting myself in the best position to have a happy home that was balanced and had good financial support to raise a child. I was very thankful for all I accomplished, and I learned quickly I couldn't do it all. My first option for daycare was within my parents' home daycare. My thoughts were at least he could be with grandparents instead of someone I didn't know. My parents owned a small home daycare since I was a teen and they remained in business at the time. Mahalek attended my parents' home daycare until he was close to three years old.

Mahalek did well there, and he was able to spend time with his cousins who attended along with him. There were a few things he did that seemed odd, but were attributed to him being away from home, such as prolonged temper tantrums and refusal to eat certain foods. For instance, my mom would tell me about how he would throw food off the highchair every day, but would eventually eat finger foods such as chicken nuggets. I thought maybe he seemed entertained at the fact someone was willing to bend down to pick up what he dropped and turned it into a game. I really thought he just wanted attention. This was not something he typically did at home, so I gave him some time to get used to eating somewhere else. Then I was told about his temper tantrums. He would eventually calm down with distraction such as a music toy or interaction with adults. As he got more comfortable, the temper tantrums were prolonged, and it took more effort to calm him down. The temper tantrums that were a little more difficult to get under control and the refusal to eat or throw food off the table remained a constant theme when he was with my parents. They were able to handle it, because he was their grandchild, and they didn't seem bothered or concerned about it.

As time passed it was apparent that Mahalek had a thing with different food textures. I remember going to eat breakfast at Cracker Barrell one morning and ordering Mahalek pancakes. When the plate came out a little bit of syrup dripped on the table and touched his hands, he immediately started flapping his fingers and making noises. At that time, we were out to eat with family who found his behavior a bit odd and dramatic. I quickly wiped his fingers and reassured him. He was so distraught about syrup being in his hands and was fixated on it. This made him frustrated for a while until the syrup was wiped off. I then noticed at home he would flare up depending on the texture of things such as sticky substances. I just thought he didn't like things sticking to his fingers and didn't really think it was odd at that time just a preference of his. I didn't really know the root cause of why the certain food textures bothered him either, I adjusted and went along with it.

As Mahalek approached his third birthday he was placed in a Society Place to help prepare for school and have social interaction with his peers. The Society Place was chosen based on a recommendation by a family friend who also had a child who attended and was around Mahalek's age. I went to tour the facility and spoke with the Director. I had a good feeling about the place and trusted the recommendation, so I enrolled him. His transition to Society Place was around the same time I started working at a university about 50 miles from home. He seemed to do well there for the first month he attended. There were not a lot of reports I received that he had any problems there.

After he got adjusted to Society Place a few weeks later, my older brother passed away. As my brother's funeral arrangement was made, I noticed when it was time to drop Mahalek off to Society Place he would run to the other side of the car and not want to get out. I was so emotionally drained and disconnected from grieving the loss of my brother, I didn't pick up on the fact that this was odd behavior. I thought maybe he felt that I was hurting and didn't want to leave me. He continued to resist getting out of the car for the next week. One day when I went to pick him up the Director briefly mentioned that he's been having a rough time lately and she thinks he may be autistic. Then a few moments later, after I picked him up and she saw who Mahalek was, she mentioned that she had made a mistake, and her comments were about another child. This was the first time I had heard, even if by mistake, Mahalek may have autism.

I began to really think about Mahalek's behaviors during his drop off times and wondered how he was being treated at Society Place. Sometimes I would drop in to check on him just to reassure him and see if there was anything going on. I began to pay even more attention to Mahalek's behaviors at home and asked the workers about how the day went each time I picked him up. It wasn't until I became curious and started asking questions that the day care facility revealed what really was going on. Then one day I learned that he had a change in teachers a few weeks ago and I wasn't notified. Then I was told that he didn't engage with other children and often threw tantrums when others were around. Suddenly, the workers and now Director were reporting everything all at once including his refusal to eat certain foods and tossing food off his plate which was consistent with what my parents reported. I experienced so many emotions when everything came out but the one that was most apparent was anger. During the reports and trying to process my feelings, the Director mentioned that he may be autistic and that I may need to consider another place for him in the future. When she mentioned it this time, I knew it wasn't a mistake and was meant for Mahalek. I had a hard time conceptualizing the idea of him being autistic and I was so upset they just sprung everything on me all at once.

This was the first time I started to feel defeated and I was in denial about the possibility of Mahalek being autistic. I just felt like Society Place didn't want Mahalek there anymore because they felt like he was too much trouble. On top of that they made it seem like his behavior was abnormal and I felt like they had a very low tolerance when it came to Mahalek. For instance, I could tell during drop-off and pick-up that they did not want to have anything to do with Mahalek and were dismissive. I began looking for other places for Mahalek to attend as I wasn't in a position where I could remove him just yet. I became more enraged just thinking about my perceptions of his treatment and decided to approach the Director about my experiences and how Mahalek's excitement for coming there had dwindled. She was receptive to my concerns at that time and then the next day, I was told by the Director that they couldn't care for him anymore based on his behavior. They didn't notify me of anything throughout the day, or check in with me, which made me more irritated. It was all told to me when I went to pick him up. Luckily, I had been placed on the waitlist at University Childcare which was located on the university campus next to the building I worked in. Around the time I was notified he could not return, University Childcare let me know there was a spot open for him. In the next few weeks, I got him placed in the University Childcare. Not only was he a few buildings away from me but I also received an employee discount so that made it much easier financially. As he made the move to a different facility, I couldn't help but think about the possibility of Mahalek showing signs of autism.

    I started to pay a little closer attention to things. There were some things that were consistent in what was reported from the Society Place such as him not engaging with his peers and only wanting to interact with adults. I began to reflect on his second birthday party at Chuck E. Cheese's. There were at least six to seven children in attendance that day. Most of the children there were his cousins and close friends. I didn't remember him really engaging with those children who attended his party or any children at Chuck E. Cheese's in general. However, he interacted well with all adults and that was his preference. I thought this behavior was happening because he was an only child and was used to dealing with adults most of the time. As I compared it to current times, these were becoming common themes for Mahalek in social settings and with that I still wasn't totally accepting of the fact that these behaviors were consistent with autism. In addition to him not engaging with his peers, he remained a very picky eater and had his preferences with food textures. The only difference at home when it came to food was that he didn't toss food off the table. I believe that was mainly because he was fed with his preferences.

University Childcare included a preschool to help him get accustomed to peers and preparation for a school like environment. I was hopeful that this would help expand his interaction with others outside of adults. University Childcare was affiliated with the university I was working in at the time which made it so much easier to manage. This brought me a lot of comfort. Knowing he was within walking distance and, if needed, I could check in on him during my breaks. He was well received by the childcare workers. He struggled a bit with verbal communication mainly due to the number of ear infections. As he got used to University Childcare, he not only began to show interest in playing with others, but his vocabulary started to expand a bit.

He loved going to the infant room which became his safe place since it was a quieter environment. This room was next to the bathrooms that he visited frequently as he was still in the process of being potty trained. University Childcare was very structured, and he fell right into the groove of things. One of his barriers was nap time. He was set up to take a nap on a cot in the toddler room with about ten other peers. Although taking naps at home was not a problem, he refused to sleep at University Childcare. His resistance to naps made him more irritable and more defiant in the afternoon. I brought his favorite blankets to use as a comfort item to help him become more comfortable sleeping at University Childcare. He was very easily distracted by some of the other kids during nap time and would often try to get up and go to the infant room. This eventually led to him getting in trouble with his teachers for not following the rules and being disruptive.

Eventually they decided not to fight the battle and let him take naps in the infant room with the intent of transitioning him back into the toddler area.

The following year he was moved into the pre-school program as a three-year-old. The first few weeks of the program, he started to have issues sharing toys with peers and taking turns on the playground equipment during playtime. He had a difficult time adjusting to things required for the school program and just preferred to play like he did before. Mahalek was an only child and he had a very hard time taking turns with others. On the other hand, he was a fast learner and did very well with school activities such as identifying numbers, shapes, letters, and colors. As a toddler he often watched educational YouTube videos about songs centered around numbers, shapes, letters, and colors so this was familiar to him. He caught on to those concepts quickly and was able to move to the next thing. The teachers often commented on how smart and advanced he was at the time.

Mahalek began to have some issues in pre-school during times of transition like when play time was over and they moved to school activities. For instance, every morning there was about an hour when he could just play and then the program started with circle time. He looked forward to playing with the toys even if it was primarily by himself. He would be excited to see all the teachers at the beginning of the day and even more excited to play with the toys, which made drop off time go smoothly. However, when circle time started, he was not a fan. I was unaware of what circle time entailed at that time. When I learned what took place and that children sang songs to learn school concepts which sometimes involved dancing, I didn't think Mahalek would have a hard time with it.

Circle time was when I noticed a pattern in his behaviors and was told he would run out of the room and scream. He typically ran to a person which was the infant room teacher or Director in the front office. They would quickly embrace him, console him, and distract him with other activities until circle time was over. They figured he just needed time to get used to the new activity or the program in general. Then it became a regular occurrence, and it became more difficult to console or calm him down. This is when they started to bring it to my attention. I didn't really know what to think of it at the time. Not only was it unusual behavior and different from what he did at home, I didn't know why he was doing it. Finally, I decided to have University Childcare let me know when circle time started so I could adjust my schedule and observe him. I did this unannounced and just watched through a window without Mahalek noticing me so I could see how he reacted. I remained undetected, because if Mahalek saw me throughout the day he would want to leave, and his separation anxiety would be at an all-time high if I left. I learned that the hard way and made sure if I made my presence known, he could leave with me. When I looked through the window, what I saw was truly a surprise and heartbreaking.

Witnessing Mahalek behave in a way I hadn't seen before, in a different environment and him being so upset, was horrifying and heartbreaking at the same time. I was terrified because I knew that this was a problem, but I didn't know how to address it at the time. I saw him scream uncontrollably and run out of the room in pure terror while the other children continued with circle time. I hadn't seen him run away from anything like that before. I could tell from watching him that he was scared and overwhelmed. Now I knew about his feelings of being overwhelmed. However, that was typically because of noises or a lot of people. In this case, the music wasn't loud and there weren't that many children, so it left me feeling very confused. I was unsure of how to help him. Here I was a registered nurse who was the Director of the program, yet I didn't know how to help my own child. I felt helpless and talked with the teachers to see if they had any ideas of possible solutions. I just felt like I was out of my depth. That day it was so hard to see him that way. I wanted to just console him as we figured out how to help. I decided to take him with me for the rest of the day. Luckily, I was able to take him back to the office for a few minutes while I wrapped up what I was doing for work prior to heading home. When he got to my office, he was very receptive and interactive with my co-workers. It was a very different behavior than what I saw during the program and it was like he returned to how he typically acted at home.

Mahalek continued to struggle with circle time even with adjustments made and became aggressive with the teachers and his peers. For instance, I remember being called when Mahalek tried to throw the computer monitors in the common area. He was throwing a tantrum because he didn't want to participate in circle time and couldn't go into the infant room. I was called and told I needed to pick him up for the day. I was so worried about what had happened I wrapped up the class I was teaching, notified my supervisor, and got there quickly. As I entered the center, I was immediately greeted by one of his preschool teachers and the Director. They had Mahalek settled and in a hallway to calm down. When he saw me, he immediately ran to me for me to pick him up and just cried in my arms. The Director and his teacher explained that he was in circle time. He had become upset from the kids singing and lost it. He began running out, hitting everyone, and then turned to things in the classroom, pushing things off the shelves and trying to throw away computer monitors. The staff at the center were concerned, and really wanted to help Mahalek be successful in the program, so we had our first discussion on what could be done differently to help him adjust. During the conversation, the Director mentioned that she suggested he get evaluated for his behavior so that they would be able to meet his needs. She thought he may have an activity deficit or hyperactivity disorder (ADHD) or autism. When I heard autism, my heart dropped, and I knew at that time that something was different with Mahalek. I slowly became more receptive to the idea of taking him to get evaluated so I took him to his pediatrician and was referred to a psychologist to get him evaluated.

In the meantime, while waiting to get him scheduled for a psychological evaluation, I noticed the temper tantrum's increased in duration at home and I even had begun to have trouble calming him down. Not only did the frequency increase when he threw a tantrum, it lasted for a while and was a bit extreme. Typically, the tantrum was when he was trying to communicate something or just got overwhelmed. He was so young he didn't have the vocabulary to say what was going on so I felt like I was playing a guessing game about what the problem could be. His communication was also delayed because of his previous ear infections. He had several hearing screens done that came back normal, so it was assumed that ear infections impacted his verbalization. When we went to public places, and I couldn't get him to calm down, I would have to leave the environment and put him in the car to get him to relax. The first tantrum he had at home that I noticed on another level was when he couldn't get his way with something and just reacted aggressively. He left very little room to respond before he went right into a meltdown. To keep myself somewhat at ease, I closed his bedroom door to decrease stimuli and give him a chance to calm down. When I began to walk away, I heard a lot of banging and a huge crash. I quickly opened the door. This was one of the first times Mahalek had become destructive at home. He was crying uncontrollably, hitting things, screaming, and just took off running. I really thought he was going to tip the dresser over and the TV was going to fall on him. All I could do was pick him up and hold him to try to get him to calm down. This was the beginning of the many holds I ended up putting Mahalek in to get him to calm down. I was so shocked at his reaction. The destruction was emotionally overwhelming and exhausting. I just felt so out of control and unable to help Mahalek. By that time, I was ready for the psychological evaluation because I wanted answers.

When his psychological evaluation was scheduled I was so nervous about what would be revealed. Even though I was receptive to the possibility of it, I couldn't help but worry about the stigma within our community regarding mental and behavioral issues. It wasn't something that was acknowledged or discussed openly. This created some anxiety about how our family would react to Mahalek and how accepting they would be. On the other hand, I wanted to know how to help my child and that outweighed anything else. I accepted the fact that if the results revealed something was wrong at least it was a step in the right direction to determine how to address it. By this time, I was so exhausted from having to pick him up from childcare centers because he wouldn't calm down, hear about him having a rough day in general, or wrestling with managing things at home I was open to whatever I needed to do to help him and alleviate those feelings.

The psychological evaluation process was a learning experience within itself. The process was long and tedious. However, the psychologist was very experienced and welcoming. Throughout each step things were explained and for the most part Mahalek did well with the evaluation. It took a few weeks for the psychologist to get the results back based on the parent assessments, observations, and other resources that were used to evaluate his behaviors. When the evaluation was scheduled, I experienced a variety of emotions. The main one was fear. Fear of the unknown and what road this would lead to. During the evaluation, it was explained that because he was only three years old the evaluation was not as clear as it could have been. We had to return about a month later to review the findings. The results revealed Mahalek had a developmental delay, mainly in speech, and mild Autism.

As soon as I heard the diagnosis, I checked out. With my nursing experience, even in pediatrics, I was so unprepared, overwhelmed, and not sure of how to proceed. After I pulled myself together I began asking several questions for clarification and directions on what to do next. The things I remember at that time to follow up on as first steps was to notify the school district to initiate an individualized education plan (IEP) to start free speech therapy aligned with his developmental delays, to explore

Applied Behavioral Analysis (ABA) therapy programs from the recommended list and use the evaluation paperwork that confirmed his diagnosis to explore other autism support services that were available. When the dust settled, I couldn't help but feel guilt and shame. I blamed myself for Mahalek's diagnosis. I thought maybe it was something I did while I was pregnant that caused it. Even though I knew better from my training, I still felt so guilty.

To be honest, I thought finally understanding why Mahalek behaved the way he did would bring me some comfort and peace with what was next. Over time, it did. However, at that time I wallowed in feelings of guilt and shame from thinking I did something wrong. There was nothing he did or could ever do for that matter that would make me feel ashamed to be his mother or not accept him. The love I had for him outweighed the thought of that and I fully embraced every difference he had. I decided to learn what I needed to do to correct the mistake or manage it from what I felt like I had contributed to at the time. I struggled with these feelings for a few years after Mahalek's diagnosis before I gave myself some grace. Most of the time I felt alone with my thoughts and feelings about how to best manage Mahalek and what really caused his differences. There was no one who truly understood what I felt. I feel into the pattern of trying to explain and validate my feelings to others and grew resentful when I was met with their inability to understand my perspective. When I began to accept the reality that some people wouldn't understand my perspective no matter what I said I put my feelings aside and remained present for what Mahalek needed. I was determined to do what was necessary to help him thrive and develop as a functioning child despite his newly documented challenges.

I embraced what the journey would bring and became more eager to learn more about autism. I started researching articles and resources for hours until I fell asleep at night. Learning new things was what I enjoyed doing and what I immersed myself in order to cope. I wanted to become efficient at managing his behaviors so I could help him and help others understand him. The first learning curve was what ABA therapy included. As a registered nurse and nurse educator, I was familiar with mental health concepts and treatments in a broad sense. I was also familiar with managing mental health and behavioral issues within the clinical setting that included autism. However, these additional community resources specific to autism were all new to me. Learning about ABA therapy was a bit scary, but refreshing, because it gave me the ability to justify my reasoning for embracing mental health and behavioral health issues to help Mahalek.

The first ABA company that was used was home based. The intent of ABA therapy was to find out what his triggers were and what strategies worked best to manage them. I was a bit uncomfortable with strangers arriving at my home to purposefully trigger Mahalek to determine what therapeutic approaches were appropriate. I struggled watching him get upset and then tried to work with him to calm him down. At times, I chose to go to another room or was filled with anger after they left for the day. There were also times I just wanted to intervene and stop treatment because I didn't see its effectiveness at the time. Eventually, the therapist moved to clinic-based services that weren't too far from where we lived. This made it easier for me to allow them to work with Mahalek since I wasn't present. During the process of working with the ABA company there was required parent training that was scheduled monthly. It gave me something to look forward to learning about. As time went on, I felt like the parent training became redundant. The information given was reinforced, but sometimes made me feel like my parenting skills were being questioned and not good enough. Sometimes I felt like they were dismissive of the information I knew about Mahalek.

The more comfortable Mahalek got with the ABA therapists the behaviors seen at Society Place and University Childcare resurfaced. He was assigned a therapist one-on-one, so it was easier for them to help manage him when he escalated. The ABA center also had a calming area where he went to work through his feelings. Before he had the option to go to a client space in public he typically ran to where he designated it as his safe place. During his time in ABA, as his triggers were explored, he became more aggressive at home with unexpected changes, overstimulation, or loud noises. I remember placing him in a hold and fighting to hold back tears as I tried to calm my child. I used the strategies they taught at first, then visual charts and timers with reminders to help with changes. I will admit, not only was it challenging to gain control of my emotions, but also my response to his reactive exacerbated behaviors. Often it would make me anxious and upset too. So now we're both upset, anxious, and trying to calm down together during his hold. At times placing him in a hold seemed forever and I just wanted to cry. I hated seeing my child having trouble calming down and getting so upset. I was also still in the beginning phases of figuring out what made him so upset. He was at an age where he couldn't really communicate his feelings which made it that much harder to identify them.

This was a very rough time for both of us. We were both learning how to navigate Mahalek's autism and trying to teach family and friends strategies along the way. Around this time, he was often sick from being exposed to other children at daycare and from his allergies. He had so many ear infections I lost count and from there he started to have breathing problems. When he was sick, it made it that much harder to distinguish his behaviors from him not feeling well versus his Autism. Trying to process what was going on and learning new things became mentally and emotionally exhausting after a while. That exhaustion made it harder to make decisions. Especially when questioned by people who didn't have a clue about what was going on or weren't open to understanding our situation. My family had a difficult time just acknowledging the fact that Mahalek had autism and that he required different approaches. A lot of times older family members tried those same strategies they used with raising their children or from the past thinking it would help Mahalek straighten up. To be honest some of those approaches just made it worse. He would just become more anxious, fearful, and withdrawn. Typically, when he didn't respond as expected, there was blame placed on me as a parenting issue versus the reality that things needed to be done differently based on Mahalek's challenges. These made me feel even more isolated with Mahalek and I became more determined to be a safe person for him. At the time, I didn't know what that looked like. I just wanted him to know I accepted every part of him no matter what and wanted him to know that he had no limits in his capacity in the world regardless of what others thought.

Chapter 4: What I Learned From the Early Signs and Resources Used

What I Learned from the Early Signs

I learned how to pay attention to the signs of when he got overstimulated or overwhelmed. When he was diagnosed with autism it just confirmed my feelings prior to his diagnosis so I became more aware of everything. I made note of situations that I felt contributed to overstimulation or aggressive behaviors. I worried so much about him and how he managed his feelings when he wasn't with me and how he would respond to new environments. It led to my development of anxiety. Currently, I still anticipate his unexpected behaviors and how I plan to address them even when he has good days. That anticipation has become a part of my subconsciousness. I often debated changing jobs or adjusting my work schedule to help alleviate that anxiety and be available when he did have a meltdown. I tried my best to be available to help him in any way I could. The fear I had about him not having the support and not being able to fully communicate his needs made me that much more anxious. I did my best to communicate my feelings the best way I could to those around me at the time. Despite my best efforts, I became very frustrated with the lack of understanding and receptiveness of others based on what I was trying to express. This made me very hesitant about having my son around people who weren't receptive because I didn't think they would be able to address his needs appropriately and would hinder his progress. I quickly felt like my circle was shrinking and my feelings were exacerbated.

I was beginning to learn that my current village may not understand or be receptive to Mahalek's autism. I felt like I was going down a road with Mahalek where I would have minimal support because of the lack of understanding and receptiveness people had at the time. I tried my best to expand my education of autism to identify resources to help me keep a balance. Since Mahalek wasn't quite school age yet I started to research schools and programs that may be a good fit for him outside of public school. However, the expense of programs outside of public school was a barrier along with the location which was typically out of the way to work or away from where we lived. As I learned more about resources and possible options for Mahalek, all I could focus on was the extra expenses and what I needed to do to generate the money. When I had discussions with people about my thoughts on how to proceed, they didn't see the problem. It was perceived that I was in a financial situation where I could comfortably take care of the added expenses based on my education. That perception was so inaccurate. During that time, I was the breadwinner of the family and worked multiple jobs just to make ends meet. I struggled with what I needed to do, and I didn't want Mahalek to be limited in resources because of a financial barrier. This sparked a new motivation for me to focus on ways to increase my revenue to get him what he needed, even if that meant adding another job.

I learned that there was limited representation of African Americans within the community who knew about resources, obtained them, or was even willing to acknowledge the need. As an African American, well educated woman, I was used to being underrepresented in my career field and life in general. I was aware of the mental health stigma within the African American community, and it became so much more apparent after Mahalek's diagnosis. I was motivated to learn what I needed to be an example within the community for addressing and treating a mental health diagnosis that can benefit us and our children. In the meantime, I embraced the resources I did find and those who are willing to share resources regardless of their racial background. There were times I felt misunderstood or became defensive of professionals such as ABA therapists who would offer advice on how to best meet Mahalek's needs at home because I didn't feel like they understood our family dynamics or culture. Looking back, it made me hesitant to proceed with certain providers because I didn't feel like they were receptive to what Mahalek needed or what he would face as an African American man in our society. The lack of representation just increased my anxiety about what Mahalek's future would look like. On the other hand, it sparked me to become his biggest advocate.

I had some experience with autistic children from my pediatric nursing experience. That experience and awareness was hard to tap into when I looked at things through the lens of a parent. For instance, I remember during the psychological evaluation process the doctor asking if Mahalek flapped his hands. My initial response was "no" until he showed me what that looked like and I quickly changed my response. The provider revealed that it is a common early sign of autism. That made me start reflecting on things and noticed other signs consistent with autism that Mahalek showed such as watching things spin, making repetitive noises, and responding inappropriately to social situations. He would flip his cars over and just watch the wheels spin for as long as he was allowed to watch them. On top of that he would make repetitive noises that sometimes didn't fit into the proper context, like making car noises when we weren't in the car, or his playing with a different toy.

I wrestled with the idea that I was able to pick on things easily with others as a nurse, but not so much with Mahalek, until I accepted it was hard to see with my own child because I didn't have an objective view. I was a part of his experience. As I worked through those feelings, I began to look at Mahalek's symptoms more objectively. I began to pick up on the fact that he had trouble with showing affection or reading others' emotions. There were times I just wanted to pick him up and give him a hug, but doing that when he wasn't ready would upset him. I had to wait until he wanted that touch or affection from me. I remember the family thinking he didn't want anything to do with them. Because he wasn't around them, as much as they liked, he wouldn't just automatically go up and greet them. Despite explaining the rationale, and how it was consistent with autism, it still was not well received. Mahalek opened another world for me in terms of education, resourcefulness, awareness, and resilience that I didn't think was possible.

What Resources Were Used to Identify the Early Signs

The biggest resources I used to get me through this time were more internal than external, such as being open to learn new things, acknowledging my feelings, and accepting the new reality. After completing my doctoral degree in nursing, I told myself I was done with furthering my education outside of the professional development requirements I had to maintain to keep my nursing license. I was so burnt out from school. I had spent my later teenage years and all my 20's working on completing my degrees. Now that I was done at the age of 29, I was not interested in other formal education even though I enjoyed learning. While completing my education, I felt like I had limited time to do the things I enjoyed, and I wanted to be fully present for my family and Mahalek. I learned to really be able to effectively meet Mahalek's needs. I needed to learn more about what he was going through and what to expect in the upcoming years. The professional development that I thought would be limited to my career expanded to formal and personal development to manage Mahalek's autism.

I began looking into ways to express my feelings or at least people I could express them with. I grew up in a household where children were seen and not heard. So, expressing emotions such as crying, or voicing opinions were not acceptable, and I struggled with expressing them as an adult. Although I became very expressive with the few friends I trusted and felt comfortable with, sometimes those typically manifested in anger, the underlying feelings were fear and deep sadness. It wasn't until later that I was forced to deal with my feelings, appropriately identify them, and work through them when they became a barrier helping my son address his feelings. I was able to identify that my fear of what Mahalek's road would look like and my perceptions of what knowledge I lacked increased my anxiety and caused frustration that was sometime projected onto others. The sadness I felt was a deep hurt from not having the support I thought I would have from family and friends who were around me at the time. This would come out as pure anger. As time passed with counseling and developing a new circle, I realized I had surrounded myself with many emotionally unavailable people who just didn't have the capacity or understanding to support me the way I needed. I eventually made peace with that, but that wasn't until later in the journey with Mahalek. However, during the early stage I had only just begun to identify how these feelings made it harder for me to determine how to proceed with Mahalek.

I began to accept the new reality that Mahalek will have to go about things in a nontraditional sense, especially with school. It was apparent that his inability to communicate and emotionally regulate posed problems with who would be able to work with him and be patient in the process. The aggressive behaviors that were a result of his inability to express or verbalize his emotions took away from the focus of academics. He was in childcare settings with the emphasis on keeping him emotionally regulated and academics were typically overlooked. I made it a point to focus on academics every chance I got so he would stay at the appropriate level. I didn't want him left behind or starting in a deficit. I was concerned about the potential of his academics suffering because of his behaviors even though he was more than capable of being academically sound. This is what made me even more receptive to getting him the appropriate resources early on to give him a foundation for school when he got to that age.

Chapter 5: Early Stages Of Finding the Right Resources

Mahalek continued in ABA therapy with the same company until he was close to four-years-old. As he got older, he began to have more issues with the setting and employees there based on the recent turnover. When the employees changed, he had a flare up in meltdowns with the transition and this time the new employees were not as friendly or as patient as the previous ones. I could tell the shift in Mahalek with him becoming more defiant and wanting to come home more so than previously. I had a funny feeling about what was really being reported to me and was not pleased with the Director's responses to my concerns. There was a time I went to a parent meeting after we returned from a short trip. Mahalek's meltdowns were more frequent and harder to control. When the Director reported this to me, I was shocked because it was a change in how he had acted before. During her presentation of his data trends, she could tell I was getting frustrated and just smirked at me. The behaviors reported were something that I had been told about only in the meeting and not as they had occurred. As I was questioning their methods and timely reporting of the recent data, her response was for him to see a psychiatrist for medication. I was so upset at the time. Not only did I have a gut feeling that something else was going on, but something did not sit right with me when it came to the Director and her intention with Mahalek's treatment plan. I was very resistant to the thought of giving him medications and felt that other options should be explored. Shortly after that parent meeting, the decision was made to remove him from that ABA center and look for different resources.

ABA therapy was not entirely bad, although my interactions and experiences with staff weren't the greatest. Mahalek had made some progression with the resources that were created for him at the time. He was introduced to the use of a timer to help with transitions. At first this started with visual charts until it was discovered he liked the sound of a timer. There were times he was so fixated on the sound that he lost track of the purpose of it, but it was helpful with transitions. When it was determined that Mahalek had a difficult time with transitions it made since following a routine was effective for him. When he heard a timer or was warned about upcoming transitions from activities he began to respond in a more relaxed state. He still resisted at times based on the activity. That resistance led to him learning how to ask for more time and if he accepted the answer, either way, he was rewarded to reinforce that behavior. ABA therapy initiated the discussion and passed along handouts that were educational resources to inform the family about how to help manage Mahalek's symptoms. This was something I was happy about and that they would be more receptive to third party information from valid sources. As information was passed along to families, I started to feel a bit at ease because I thought maybe the resistance to what I passed was because of some personal reason. I figured third party information was best since it included an expert's recommendation. When the information was presented and not received appropriately it just confirmed their difficulty with accepting Mahalek's reality. I felt even more limited to who I could truly trust with Mahalek. I wanted Mahalek to feel accepted and loved. In addition to that, I wanted him to be treated fairly.

Shortly after ABA services were stopped for a brief time, he was placed in special pre-kindergarten for speech therapy at the elementary school within the school district. This was a program he could go to for help with speech according to the delays indicated on his initial psychological evaluation. The first step with getting him started was a speech evaluation. Even though the psychologist went over the results I was still a bit unclear of what speech issues Mahalek had. Mahalek was receptive to the communication methods we used at home. At times, I did notice he began to have trouble following two-step instructions, but I thought it was because of his age. I knew at the time he was a little delayed in using words or responding verbally to certain things. Mahalek was engaged and enjoyed working with the speech therapist. He had one-hour sessions with her weekly. He tried to run a few times, when he didn't agree with some of the exercises, but it wasn't as bad as what he did in other childcare settings. During his speech sessions, I was present to help as needed, which made it a little easier to get him to comply. After his evaluation the speech pathologist mentioned that there will be goals listed the following year on the Individualized Education Plan (IEP) to keep services going. This was the first time I had heard of these goals needing to go on an IEP or the potential need for an IEP to start the upcoming school year. Overall, the special pre-kindergarten speech was effective in helping him with the beginning stages of communication and transitioning into that school environment.

Based on Mahalek's struggles with multiple ear infections and possible contribution to his delayed speech along with his breathing issues I stayed in close contact with his doctor. He was referred for hearing screens and an evaluation to see if he needed tympanostomy tubes placed. His hearing screens came back good and the doctor who evaluated him for tubes decided he didn't need them unless he had more infections. After the evaluation, he didn't have any more ear infections. However, he began to have more difficulty with his breathing. I remember Mahalek struggling to breathe and staying up all night trying to breathe or reposition himself. I tried every over-the-counter remedy to help him including the use of essential oils, which was helpful for a short period of time. I decided to take him to urgent care since he did not improve and found out he had strep and pneumonia. They had a hard time keeping his oxygen levels up even though he was given multiple breathing treatments at the time. We ended up having to be transported to the emergency room (ER). He ended up stabilizing and we discharged with an albuterol inhaler and steroids. After discharge from the ER, Mahalek followed up with his primary care physician and it was determined that his symptoms were consistent with asthma. His asthma was triggered with changes in the barometric pressure and seasonal allergies. The challenges he had with ear infections and asthma exacerbated his autism symptoms. Sometimes, his medical conditions masked his autism symptoms and made it that much harder to determine the cause and triggers of his behaviors.

Mahalek's autism had its challenges, but there were also good things that came with it as well. I started to recognize the beauty in Mahalek's differences, and I was thankful to experience them. The level of comfort he had developed in his own differences as a young child was refreshing and inspiring. I knew that as he grew older the world may not be so accepting and I wanted him to develop confidence in himself. He was very aware and seemed to have a photographic memory. For instance, he loved cars and knew the details of every car he was exposed to. He knew every make and model of cars, family, and friends along with his teachers, neighbors, and people he met along the way. This evolved into him verbalizing every make and model of car he had seen on the road. I remember asking him on several occasions if he recognized cars in the parking lot based on who were meeting or visiting at the time. I knew if he had seen their car and let me know that it was time to go in or that person had arrived. This became a topic he was often fixated on and sometimes deferred to if he wasn't interested in the present conversation. There were so many people who were impressed by his knowledge of cars. I would find myself asking him if he would build me a car one day based on his interest and impressive recognition of cars.

There were times that his fascination with cars led to other things that were a bit scary with his poor perception of safety. For instance, when he was overwhelmed or scared, he would often run with no destination in mind just to escape whatever was triggering him. Sometimes it ended up with him running in the road or getting in a stranger's car. I remember him running out of the front door and when I screamed his name for him to come back, he got more upset and ran faster to get into a stranger's car. Once, I was able to chase him down and stop him from getting in the car, he calmed down and I began reinforcing concepts of stranger danger. I didn't understand until much later that me raising my voice contributed to his anxiety and often made it more difficult for him to calm down. Then there were times he just ran for attention and to see who would chase him. On the other hand, when he recognized my voice, he often hesitated to run very far once he heard it. He didn't like being out of my sight for long and the anxiety of thinking he was lost would stop him. I worked hard to start being more aware of my emotional state, which led to me to prioritize my mental and emotional wellbeing, so I could respond in a more peaceful state.

Mahalek was introduced to extracurricular activities that could help with his anxiety and emotional regulation. I learned about a music class designed for children with special needs at the local sensory gym. One positive factor was the fact that the music teacher was male and Mahalek tended to stay calmer when dealing with males versus females. I went ahead and got him enrolled. During music class, Mahalek showed an interest in playing the piano. At first things started out well. He was fascinated with the instrument itself and the sounds it made. I figured this would be a good place to start, as far as an extracurricular activity, that it was something he could participate in alone. He always showed an interest in listening to music. On the other hand, he was not fond of listening to people sing or dance for recreation, that typically led to some type of meltdown. As he got more comfortable with piano lessons, there were some days he started to rebel against the instructor's schedule and lessons presented. His fixation on other things in the studio and the difficulty with transitioning from preferred activities detoured his interest in the piano at times. Sometimes he wanted to look at the other instruments or play with the speakers versus learning the know-how's of playing the piano. The instructor began to get creative with breaks and incentives that worked for the most part unless Mahalek was just having a bad day. In those cases, we just called it a day early and let him be. Another barrier to his compliance with music lessons some days was the fact that he wanted to play in the gym itself. To get to the music room, we entered through the main entrance and walked through the gym. It was suggested I begin parking in the back of the gym and enter that way so he wouldn't be distracted. We went to music class as scheduled and his reward was to play in the gym afterwards.

Mahalek started pre-kindergarten shortly after he started music lessons. I was excited for him to start school and a bit nervous at the same time. I was anxious anticipating what the discussions about his IEP would be and how to prepare for the meeting. I was also concerned about his teacher's ability to handle his behaviors and the possible lack of tolerance with Mahalek's meltdowns despite their reassurance. I remember going to the back-to-school night and meeting the teachers who were so welcoming. I told them about Mahalek's behaviors and what tended to work for him with the help of the ABA tools and training I received. I made it a point to share strategies that may help if he gets upset such as how he needed a safe place, assistance with transitions, and how to help him minimize the sounds to decrease the risk of him running away with he heard them. I was under the impression that the advice I was giving them was preparing them in the best way to be able to deal with his behaviors. I anticipated it may be a transition that I had to assist with which is why I left my job at the university and found one closer to home to be nearby if needed.

Within the first week or so of him starting pre-kindergarten an IEP meeting was scheduled. I didn't have much exposure to or knowledge of the process prior to that meeting. I was just excited that everyone was willing to meet to discuss the best ways to help Mahalek in school. The meeting was brief and we discussed goals that would be helpful for him to succeed. The goals were mainly geared toward speech since at that time he had problems with his receptive and expressive communication. I emphasized the things that had happened in childcare centers which led to him having meltdowns. I wanted to make sure they were aware of the potential that he may be aggressive and run away from them. They seemed to be understanding about the information I was giving them. As we wrapped up the meeting and I informed them of things that we learned with ABA therapy that were helpful with transitions and overstimulation, I thought we were at a good place and that things would run a bit smoother. I expected them to have the proper training and experience, to be able to deal with Mahalek, only to find out that was very unrealistic.

After the second week of starting pre-kindergarten, I had already received a few calls within hours of him starting the school day. One of the worst feelings, when you receive a call that your child is having problems, is picking up on the teacher's frustration and anxiety. I have always been anxious from the anticipation of what the childcare centers, ABA therapists, and now school would tell me Mahalek was doing. However, sensing that frustration from the teachers was very different. By the time I made it to the school, the defeat, frustration, and sometimes disgust from his behaviors was very apparent. I understood the emotional, mental, and physical toll it took to get Mahalek calmed down. As a mother I was very apprehensive to the thought of someone else's frustration potentially being harmful to my child.

My feelings about Mahalek potentially being harmed in childcare or school settings stemmed from the treatment at the childcare centers. My personal experiences with abuse made it that much worse. I understood not everyone accepted Mahalek's challenges or was willing to do the things necessary to help him with them. Prior to his placement in the pre-kindergarten class, for half days at the elementary school, I had reviewed options with the school for the best class placement. Since there were limited spots for him in pre-kindergarten and he was enrolled in a special pre-kindergarten, they opened the option to place him in another school within the district that included a special needs classroom. One day I went to tour the classroom which had a teacher to student ratio of 1:10 and two teachers. As it got closer to enrollment day, the school decided to place him in a regular classroom, with a student teacher ratio of 1:20, with the option for him to go to a resource room if needed. The school in our district didn't have a special education teacher unless he was in the fourth grade which meant the teachers in the lower grade levels had limited support with special needs children. When Mahalek started to have problems in school I was confused as to why he wasn't placed in the class with lower ratios initially. I understood every bit of frustration the teachers had in trying to figure out what worked but what I refused to tolerate was mistreatment. As a victim of abuse, I was triggered at the thought of Mahalek having to experience any unfair treatment.

I noticed that Mahalek began to withdraw at home after he was in school for a few weeks. This was abnormal because he was very engaged and happy at home or typically returned to that state after he returned home from having a tough day in childcare or school. However, I just knew something was different and he was struggling internally. We had family over one day and typically Mahalek would rush to the living room to see who was present, even if it was just to stare or mention something off topic. However, this time he was not engaged. I sat back and watched him stay to himself and he really looked depressed. I knew that it stemmed from how he was treated in school and that something different needed to be done. His perceptions of how he was treated during meltdowns or the trouble he had during school were affecting him at home. Some of the children were allowed to bully him and exclude him based on how he acted. He needed a safe place and safe people at school. At that time I just knew something wasn't right and I didn't feel like public school was a good fit.

During my drive to work I began to think about what the best option for Mahalek would be, as far as school, with teachers who have the training to deal with his symptoms. I had a lecture scheduled that morning. Immediately after I finished teaching, I started to research other school opportunities for Mahalek. I just didn't think public school was a good fit and it was in my heart to do something about it. I thought maybe he needed to be in a place where he was around kids with similar needs and with teachers who understood how to care for those needs. I really felt like if his environment wasn't welcoming of his differences, not only would his mental and emotional state suffer, but so would his academics. I looked around and stumbled upon a charter school that had one-to-one instruction including an assigned teacher with a curriculum that resembled a homeschool format. I felt confident that was a good step, especially at such a young age. To help get him a better educational foundation, in an environment he was receptive to, until he got to a good age to handle the public school environment. I went ahead and submitted all the documentation to get him enrolled over my lunch break. I was unaware that submitting enrollment paperwork would notify the existing school immediately of his enrollment elsewhere. I received a phone call from the school he was currently attending within one hour of his enrollment submission at the charter school. The public school was calling to check with me and thought it was a mistake. When I confirmed that the enrollment was intentional the school seemed disappointed, but respected my decision. I thought this was the best decision for Mahalek. Looking back, I may not have given the public school enough time to adjust to Mahalek. I just wasn't willing to take the risk of sacrificing Mahalek's mental and emotional wellbeing while they were adjusting.

I had learned a little about the homeschool processes from discussions with other mothers at the sensory gym Mahalek played in and attended music lessons. My primary job was in higher education, so I felt prepared enough to learn how to manage Mahalek's schooling. I understood the curriculum from a higher education perspective, and I was eager to learn it from a K-

12 perspective. I felt a bit of ease knowing he would be assigned to a teacher within the district that would meet with him weekly and facilitate his schoolwork. This worked out great initially with him being able to complete his schoolwork at home with breaks. I had the option to help with completing his work around my work schedule and schedule the weekly meetings at home. The work he had to complete wasn't too time consuming in pre-kindergarten. We would be able to spend a few hours a day and do projects such as arts and crafts on the weekend to keep him on pace. Mahalek was great with this teacher until he got comfortable and then started to be a little defiant. Since meetings were at home, I was able to intervene and help him refocus and comply with her instructions. His resistance and short attention span were a big part of his inability to comply and follow instructions. We started breaking the time frame up into smaller chunks and gave him breaks to help him get through his work. I began looking into ways to keep him engaged and more receptive to school instruction.

The teacher he had with the charter school felt a little threatened with my participation in trying to assist Mahalek with staying on task during her instruction. There were times I just stayed out of the way until it got to the point where she couldn't get him under control. I passed along information learned in the ABA parent meetings, along with evidence-based practice strategies I was familiar with in higher education, to explore as options to increase his compliance. She wasn't very open to using them and wanted to be the one who identified and addressed his needs solely. This made me angry and I felt like my parental knowledge was being dismissed. I felt like I could be helpful in the process and that some strategies needed to be modified based on Mahalek's background and needs. Mahalek is a very smart child, but sometimes that is manifested in ways that may not be ideal. For instance, he would study a person's mannerisms and figure out what he could get away with. The minute you were inconsistent he would meltdown in attempts to get you to respond the way he wanted. This made it that much more important to maintain as consistent a routine as possible. In addition to a consistent routine, a consistent approach of handling his behaviors, with all individuals in all settings, was essential.

I did what I knew best and investigated academic programs and other educational options in hopes that people would take my feedback about Mahalek seriously. I just needed to figure out a way to communicate my thoughts with his teachers where they would be receptive. On top of that I decided to find something that would link to some sort of credential that would be helpful in validating my knowledge of autism independent from being his mother. Eventually I found a certification program about autism that aligned with my existing experience and qualifications. It was a self-paced program that could be completed in less than a month, was reasonably priced, and internationally recognized. So, I decided to complete the program to learn more about autism and become an Autism Specialist. This program included information about what the IEP entailed and the process of IEP development. I didn't use the information about IEPs as quickly as I would like since Mahalek was now in a virtual homeschool format. An IEP was not necessarily required and developed in a broad sense because his teachers have limited interaction with him. I became passionate about learning how to reinforce his positive behaviors in hopes to increase his compliance and decrease those negative behaviors that led to his aggression. I was eager to learn more and remained as opened minded as I could.

As Mahalek moved to kindergarten more things surfaced that required adjustment. He was required to complete benchmark testing and attend weekly co-op meetings that included other teachers and children. When he was in pre-kindergarten the teacher came to our home and worked with him to complete his assignments. This made it easier to redirect him and de-escalate him when he resisted instructions or had meltdowns. Now with him going into kindergarten, and the changes in the structure of the meetings and testing requirements, it made it a little more difficult to manage his behaviors in public and address his anxiety with testing. When it was time for benchmark testing, he was easily distracted and sometimes just refused to do his work. He had anxiety with reading instructions and being attentive long enough to complete the test. This made it very difficult to determine Mahalek's academic performance. Sometimes he would just click on answers to complete the test to keep his anxiety down to finish quickly. To help him answer questions on the test in the most accurate way his teachers would ask me to remote in and help him keep him focused. The teacher also tried to have tests in different environments and incorporated breaks. As far as the co-op meetings he began to struggle with social interaction and exposure to some classroom formats. He was eager about going somewhere new and being around other kids. It took a while to change his perception that the meeting was for school and not a playdate. Mahalek loved attention and looked for that one-on-one instruction he was used to in ABA therapy and previous meetings with his teachers. When he realized that the teacher had to attend to all student needs, he would get upset and tried to get that one-on-one attention. This required some adjustment with my work schedule to be present during these meetings to help him understand the change and transition to it. There were days we did very well and then days I had to remove him and take him home for the day.

During his co-op meeting, he did well with individual, short sessions and played with a peer or two. He still had a difficult time with circle time or when the class sang songs or danced. Mahalek's anticipation of singing was a trigger and made it hard for him to transition to the next activity. There were times I had to carry him outside of the classroom and take him to the car when those episodes started. After he calmed down, I returned him to the classroom, when the activity was over, to finish his session. Eventually the teacher moved the time for singing and dancing to the end of the session then gave me a heads up before they started so I could leave with Mahalek. This worked better. He was able to get his schoolwork done and participate without feeling like he missed out because he couldn't handle it. I was happy I was able to make this work with my busy schedule and multiple jobs at the time. The constant adjustment and redirection made me emotionally and mentally exhausted more than I could express. I just felt like I was on autopilot during that time juggling multiple tasks for work while doing what I needed for Mahalek. Some days, to prepare for his behavior during those meetings, I disconnected and walked around in the parking lot repeatedly just to come back to myself. I had limited assistance when it came to dealing with Mahalek's meltdowns and transportation to school events.

Looking back, I'm not sure how I got through it. I relied heavily on my spiritual faith and determination to be the best mother to keep me focused.

I started looking into other things that would help keep Mahalek at ease to alleviate some of the stress of managing his behaviors. I was introduced to essential oils to help Mahalek calm down by a parent at the sensory gym. She was selling oils to help manage things such as breathing problems and to help with sleep promotion. As I began looking at the prices of the packages and what was included in each mixture, I decided it was cheaper to try to make my own. I stayed up many nights finding recipes on how to make oil blends and researching oils that have been used to calm children with autism. I ended up going to the local natural food store and asking the naturopathic doctor for the best oils to purchase to help with stress and staying calm to see which one's matched what I had researched. I made a few blends with coconut oil to help him sleep, manage his allergies, stay focused with school, stay calm prior to school or ABA, and when he had meltdowns. I used a combination of distilled water, lavender, and chamomile to spray on Mahalek's pillow to help him sleep. Then I made an oil blend with sweet orange, lavender, and vetiver that I would roll on his wrist to help him stay calm for the day. I even tried that a time or two for myself before I went to work and was very pleased how it helped me relax. There were a few others I put together, such as one for when he was in the middle of a meltdown, that I used to put on the bottom of his feet. That was very useful in decreasing the time it took him to calm down and the time I had to place him in a hold. Sometimes I forgot that I had an oil already made when he was in the middle of a meltdown, but the times I remembered it helped. As I continued to use the oils, I even used drops of oils in his bathwater such as peppermint, lavender, and chamomile to help with relaxation and his breathing.

Chapter 6: What I Learned And Resources Selected

What I Learned About the Resources

I learned that I was one of Mahalek's biggest resources and that I needed to be as knowledgeable as I could be to help advocate for him. One of the biggest challenges for me during this time was understanding the legalities and processes of an adequate IEP and how it would benefit Mahalek. I was still getting accustomed to the processes of K-12 education and the differences compared to my experiences with higher education. I was aware that his diagnosis opened him up for more options to resources. I hadn't yet explored what could be beneficial to help support him in school. His behaviors were one of the biggest barriers that delayed my ability to identify resources, because I was so consumed with that. I noticed that his behaviors may overshadow his academic needs, so I wanted to make sure it was documented appropriately with the school to make sure he stayed on track. I took the initiative to learn how to best facilitate this process to keep his academic progress on track while managing his autism symptoms. I tried my best to remain hopeful that he would be able to attend public school once he got a good foundation of how to cope with his disability with the variety of services and resources that were used around this time. I was told that public school had more resources and people to help him. I learned quicky that the time I thought I had to figure this all out came quicker than I expected.

ABA Parent Training was a great resource that shared tools that were developed or could be developed to pass along to family and the schools in addition to identifying some of his triggers. I began to understand what ABA entailed and became more open to placing him with another ABA company. That placement could help him develop social skills that would be appropriate for him to function in social settings and a school environment. My perceptions of the first ABA company were mixed. However, I learned quite a bit about resources and had some things to pass along to my family to help them understand Mahalek's needs. This helped me be able to adapt tools as he got older that were appropriate as his needs and triggers changed. This training helped open my eyes to people who had limited knowledge about autism and who were struggling to interact with Mahalek based on their lack of knowledge. I struggled in this stage with knowing that Mahalek's inclusion in the world and with others was going to be another barrier on top of him being an African American male. Despite it all, I was still determined to advocate and protect him the best way I knew how. ABA and parent training was great in finding ways to manage triggers, but not so much for identifying the underlying cause. That was something we addressed with therapy as he got older.

I was informed about Autism Speaks and the resources available within the organization. I began to investigate the resources and was a bit overwhelmed when I visited the website. One thing I noticed was the wide variety of resources and events that addressed autism from a national perspective. As I went through the events, articles, and other information presented it just seemed like a lot at once and I was mentally overwhelmed. I figured it would be best for me to start slow and sign up as an advocate to receive regular updates on things that were newly emerging for those with autism. After a while, I saw there was not too much involvement in my state compared to others. Despite reviewing the Autism Speaks website I still didn't feel like I had the best picture of what was truly out there. One thing I became excited about was the fundraising walks and other events that pulled people together with the same diagnosis. I felt like those things really highlighted the need to help those diagnosed with autism feel more functional and included in the world. I still felt like there was something else I needed to investigate, that was age appropriate for Mahalek, to help him get through the early stages.

What Resources Were Chosen

I did a lot of research and started to network to find resources appropriate for his age at the time. I remember researching so much information I would just fall asleep in the process. I was very intrigued by the potential to learn more about recent evidence that would bring me some peace with what to expect as Mahalek gets older. I read so many articles and searched for resources that were supported by evidence. During this time, I didn't really immerse myself into reading books per se because I was so burnt out from reading in academic programs. The stories I received were from people who I was referred to by word of mouth. For instance, I remember being referred to contact a mother who had an adult son with autism. I was told her son had similar struggles as Mahalek in school and with aggression. I was eager to hear how she managed everything and got him to the point where he was independent and coping effectively. The people I shared stories with at that time gave me hope that all my efforts to get my son where he needed to be would pay off and he could become functional and independent in the world. I was inspired by parents who raised children with special needs, who are now thriving, despite the messy and unpredictable journey they experienced. This was a resource that gave me more strength and understanding of what I was facing.

There were a few resources that helped Mahalek at that time. The development of a visual chart and a timer to help with transitions, along with the knowledge I received by becoming an Autism Specialist, helped to facilitate appropriate use of the tools and expand my knowledge. Mahalek's autism diagnosis was still fresh although it had been a few years. It was such a huge learning curve to figure out how to help him, sometimes I felt very isolated in my experiences. Mahalek had a hard time following more than one direction at a time and staying on task for a period, so I adapted a chart to help him. The chart I adapted was a First and Then chart that was created during ABA therapy and included laminated pictures of items or activities at home to use as incentives. These pictures were attached with Velcro to illustrate steps of what he needed to do first such as complete a worksheet and then he could play with a toy for five minutes. I used a white board with magnets and Velcro along with pictures of things Mahalek liked to make on the board. I began to loop his teacher in on how to use the board to help him with completing his schoolwork. We began to use a timer to help him with understanding when his time was up with schoolwork, when he could play, and when he had to return to his schoolwork or next task. Mahalek loves the sound of timers if it isn't too loud and sometimes he gets fixated on them going off. However, it has been one of the most effective resources to help him with transitions, especially if he received a few warnings prior to the timer going off. This helped decrease some of my anxiety and stress of finding out ways to help him maintain his focus on what the task was at the time.

The certification program to become an Autism Specialist was another great resource. After completion of the certification program, the thing that helped the most was the ongoing professional development opportunities which helped me stay up to date. I was able to show my certificate to validate the knowledge I received, and it helped some professionals become more open to my thoughts about next steps with Mahalek. The certification helped me become more comfortable in discussing things such as the pieces of an IEP and tools to help reinforce his positive behaviors. This helped me address people from a professional standpoint instead of being a protective mother immersed in my emotions. That way I could think through the processes logically to advocate for him. I was also able to identify other triggers and main behaviors and figure out ways to manage them.

While Mahalek was enrolled at the charter school I learned

about the learning fund that helped pay for extracurricular activities or school equipment needed. This helped relieve some of the financial burden and I started to use this fund for his music lessons. There was a list of places that accepted the learning funds, and I explored a few such as martial arts. Mahalek just wasn't interested or old enough at the time to take it seriously. The learning fund was also used to purchase him a computer to use for schoolwork. Although I had a computer he could use, I still purchased one from the learning fund, so I didn't have to share mine with him. This helped me out so much at the time to get him the things he needed.

Chapter 7: Homeschool and the Pandemic

During the last few months of Mahalek's kindergarten year the COVID-19 pandemic shut down was in effect. This was a huge turning point in our lives. For example, I debated on looking at different job opportunities in the past, mainly virtual. Although I had just recently started a part-time virtual position, with the demands of my full-time position, along with my part-time positions, homeschooling, and being a caregiver, I realized too much time spent at home made me feel lost and depressed. The ability to get out of the house and interact was so essential to my mental and emotional wellbeing. One thing I looked forward to during the pandemic was the ability to homeschool Mahalek without worrying about working things around my schedule or addressing issues with his difficulty in social environments. I was able to develop a schedule at home that worked well. I used my lunch break time to go for a walk or get a workout in. After the workday, I would take time to go for a quick run. Exercise was my way of coping and keeping my stress levels down. The beauty of it was that I was able to work out and incorporate that time with Mahalek as well.

The pandemic helped put things in perspective and gave me some time to slow down and think. For instance, I was so used to being on the go all the time and trying to care for everyone else besides myself. The pandemic forced me to slow down and look around. Mahalek enjoyed the time at home with my presence. I realized I had not really been able to spend as much time with him as I would've liked outside of keeping him on task with school or finding ways to help him stay at ease. I remember spending a lot of time outside with him riding bikes, letting him ride in his car while I jogged alongside him, and just taking random trips to the lake to get out of the house. The time I was able to spend with him was needed and helped put us both at ease. We had more flexibility in completing his schoolwork which took the pressure off figuring out how to get his schoolwork in. Instead of completing it primarily in the evenings when I returned home, we were able to get it done during the day and had more time to spend in the evening. Mahalek started to get used to me being home and the new normal which wasn't a bad thing. One thing I noticed was that I was in constant caregiver mode, at this point, with no breaks. Prior to the pandemic, I would go to work and be out of the environment or could focus on something else. However, while working remotely I was caregiving and working around the clock and then suddenly I got sick. I didn't have COVID-19, but it sure felt like it at the time. I couldn't do much and was very weak and sluggish for about three weeks. During that time, there wasn't anyone who stepped in to help with any of the tasks I had at home, and I was still completing them while trying to care for myself at the same time. This made me realize that something had to change for me to effectively practice self-care and have the support I really needed to sustain us. It made me think about my abilities to care for Mahalek and what care he would receive if something happened to me.

The summer of the pandemic, when the academic year was completed, I had to return to work with social distancing. The nice thing about the pandemic was the increased flexibility in attending meetings since they were switched to virtual instruction. Prior to the pandemic, I had consistently planned for Mahalek's in person speech sessions and teacher meetings. After the pandemic, they all switched to virtual format which included times that worked around my work schedule. That flexibility made it so much easier to attend meetings for Mahalek. Around this time, Mahalek began attending ABA at a new facility closer to my job. When I returned to work that summer Mahalek was able to attend ABA therapy to continue working on his behavioral and social goals. I was optimistic about him resuming ABA this time to help with some of the issues that were common themes in the social setting. I was more concerned about his aggressive behaviors and when he ran from teachers. I didn't want it to continue as he got older without trying to give him the appropriate resources. I placed him in environments with people who could help him keep those behaviors under control. As Mahalek progressed with ABA therapy, and I returned to work, a shift in our family dynamic took place. This is when Mahalek's father and I decided to file for divorce.

Mahalek was starting his first-grade year when the divorce process took place. I began to prepare for the shift of becoming a single mother and the need for additional support. I looked for places that Mahalek could attend part-time around the days he didn't attend ABA to assist with his schoolwork. I investigated childcare centers and potential caregivers that could come to our home during the day to assist. When that didn't work out, I called around to see if there were any facilities specific to children with special needs that had openings. Finally, I decided to call the owner of the sensory gym Mahalek frequently attended to see if anyone there knew of places that were recommended for children with autism or special needs in general. I was recommended to the Tutoring Center that was about ten minutes from where I lived at the time. I was very surprised to learn about the recent opening at the center that was once an accredited school for students with special needs since it was so close to the start of the school year. The owner was a previous special education teacher with a behavioral therapy background. I called her to get more information about the program and just from our brief conversation I knew this was the place for Mahalek. She was still enrolling for the school year and only had a few openings left so I quickly confirmed.

    The day for orientation at the Tutoring Center was scheduled within less than a week of the phone call. I immediately started completing all the required paperwork needed to get Mahalek started. I was excited for Mahalek to go to orientation and see how he interacted with the teacher. I remember going into the classroom the day of orientation and immediately feeling like that was the place for Mahalek. The teacher had the proper background, and the parents were so receptive since each of their children had some sort of special need. Mahalek was in a place with children he could identify with. The classroom was in a local neighborhood in the back of a residence. I was very nervous with the thought of Mahalek transitioning into somewhere new, especially with the changes at home. The parents that were present made me feel so much more optimist and Mahalek really gravitated toward the teacher and everyone in the room which let me know this was the right place for him. To this day, even though Mahalek hasn't been there in a few years, we still drop in from time to time to visit everyone and give them an update. The experiences from the prior school and child care programs were understood by the parents at the Tutoring Center and their children were there for similar reasons as Mahalek. For the first time I had found a program with children and families who shared similar experiences that led to them seeking out nontraditional methods for educating their children.

Mahalek started at the Tutoring Center, part-time for two days a week, while attending ABA therapy the other three days a week. For instance, he attended ABA therapy on Mondays, Wednesdays, and Fridays and the Tutoring Center on Tuesdays and Thursdays. The split format allowed Mahalek to get used to different places. As he had difficulties with the transition to the Tutoring Center, I still knew I would have reliable childcare with ABA, and I could loop them in on how the transition went at the Tutoring Center so those things could be addressed to help him. When the ABA therapist learned about Mahalek attending the Tutoring Center part-time they were a bit apprehensive. At the time, I didn't understand it. Later I realized they were afraid I would just leave all together and they would lose money. Mahalek had been making huge improvements with ABA and my insurance company was getting pickier with the hours he was attending since his need was decreasing. I tried my best to explain my rationale for using the

Tutoring Center as additional support to help me with Mahalek's school work and supplemental information to keep him on track academically. The other thing I brought to their attention was Mahalek's recent interest in wanting to be around other children. While in ABA therapy, although he was around children, he mainly interacted with his therapist one-on-one and was now eager to have more peer-to-peer interaction.

I was also in contact with the ABA director during our meetings about how to best address the transition and trauma Mahalek was experiencing with the divorce. Since the pandemic I had the option to attend ABA parent meetings in person or virtually. Most of the time I scheduled the meetings in-person, early in the day or at the end of the workday, since the location wasn't too far from my job. To help Mahalek and I get through this difficult time, I resumed my therapy sessions virtually. Mahalek was slowly introduced to therapy with me to help him with the exacerbation of his behaviors and anger. During all of that, we decided to sell our home and move a few months after the school year started.

The move was rapid from the increased interest in people looking for homes. We ended up selling the house within a week of placing it on the market and we were looking to move within a month. I decided to find a place close to the area we were familiar with and the Tutoring Center to maintain consistency for Mahalek. I kept Mahalek looped in on everything and included him in the process of selecting a new place, so he knew what to expect. Mahalek handled the move well and was excited to live in a new place. I thought that change would be very difficult for him, but he embraced it. He often mentioned he felt like he was coming home to a hotel every day. This was refreshing too because I knew he felt comfortable and secure. Mahalek was used to traveling and loved staying in hotels. Sometimes he would just want to stay in the hotel and play. I tried my best to maintain some normalcy during the process of changing residences. Mahalek seemed so much happier after the move. At times, he would express how he missed the old house and his dad living with us. I remained open with him as he expressed his feelings and reassured him that we would both remain active in his life and loved him no matter what. The change and move were a good thing for us both despite how difficult it was. I had come out of a situation where I was a caregiver, along with being a mother of a child with special needs, while working multiple jobs to make sure everyone was taken care of. I had entirely too much on my shoulders and the change took some of that off. Sure, I had a lot of healing to do, which was a separate journey in its own, but I was in a better space to begin to really get back in alignment and be the mother that I envisioned myself to be.

We ended up moving to a place that was about five minutes from the Tutoring Center. That gave Mahalek some time to sleep in and kept me on track with drop-off and pick-up times. The divorce was a traumatic experience for him and those at the Tutoring Center were more understanding of his situation compared to those he interacted with in ABA therapy. The ABA therapists even changed their perspective of me once they found out I was now a single mother trying to balance it all. Mahalek was looking for a new support system, just as I was, during the transition to something new.

Mahalek struggled with anger he didn't know how to express

from the divorce and the move. He started to pick up on negative behaviors he saw in the past and he would challenge women in authority, which led to an increase in aggressiveness to those he felt he could do that to. On the other hand, he was very receptive to those younger than him and wanted to protect them. He began to struggle a bit with his identity and how to appropriately interact. He also began to realize that his aggressive behavior affected how his peers interacted with him the next day or during his episodes at the Tutoring Center. This was very difficult for him to understand because he looked at it as a form of rejection versus them being frightened by his unpredictable pattern of outbursts. It wasn't until a few years later, with additional services and maturity, that Mahalek was able to verbalize his anxiety when it came to his friends not accepting him based on his past behaviors. He has come a long way and still struggles with the concept that he must show others he can be different and in control of his emotions. However, at that time he was very out of control and didn't realize the extent of his behavior until he came out of it or was shown a video of himself.

This was a very tough time for us both. I became good at hiding my emotions from him. I didn't want him to see me hurting and I thought it would make his behavior worse. Because I worked so hard to help him and be present, it increased his reliance on me to help him through his feelings and when things got overwhelming. He would say he missed me or acted up for me to come get him. He became even more attached to me and had issues with separation anxiety. He started to think I should be available for him no matter what. For instance, I remember his teacher at the Tutoring Center telling me that in the middle of the meltdown he stated he missed me and wanted me to come pick him up. At least we were able to determine his intent and find ways to work around it. We ended up doing short check-ins over FaceTime and occasionally I would talk to him if he was upset to help prevent him from having a meltdown. As time went on he continued to have problems adjusting to the environment with only attending a few days of the week. We discussed the option of him attending part-time versus full-time. Since he was still in ABA therapy, I ran the idea by his ABA therapist. The therapist was not interested in hearing about him wanting more peer interaction and the need for consistency in one place. They were resistant, but ultimately agreed to collaborate with the teacher at the Tutoring Center to see if they could provide guidance to help Mahalek settle in better.

Within a few weeks, a time was scheduled for the ABA therapist to sit in the classroom at the Tutoring Center to observe. The ABA therapist came in the morning since that's when Mahalek was the most receptive and stayed through the lunch time to see how he behaved with schoolwork. Mahalek's confidence with completing schoolwork wasn't where it should have been. He sometimes got upset with having to complete it because he thought it was too hard. Getting him to engage and try to complete schoolwork as his levels advanced became an ongoing issue. Mahalek ended up having a meltdown because he didn't want to complete his schoolwork with the ABA therapist present. I remember the teacher calling me to tell me that I needed to check on him since they could not get him to calm down. As I arrived that afternoon, while the teacher at the Tutoring Center filled me in, I noticed I got very little feedback from the ABA therapist.

There was very little intervention on her part when he got upset or with providing suggestions that may help. Mahalek had been with this company for a little over a year, so they knew him well enough to intervene appropriately. That day I was at my wits end and was so overwhelmed I just took Mahalek home with me to decompress.

As I reflected on that day, I began to really focus on what the intent of ABA therapy was for Mahalek. I was a little more assertive in meetings, trying to figure out what plan they had to help him regulate more. Then I remembered it coming out in one of the parent meetings that they did not agree with the teacher's instruction or him going to the Tutoring Center at all. I followed up with wanting to know their thoughts on other places that would be a good fit and helpful in assisting me with making sure his schoolwork was completed. I informed them that completing all schoolwork in the evening was not doable, based on the amount Mahalek had to complete, and it gave him little free time at home. I truly believe this added to everything he felt at the time, and I was fighting for a balance for both of us. Mahalek continued in the ABA center for a few months with the intent of helping transition him to public school and to work with the teachers in the district where there were far more resources. As Mahalek began to plateau in ABA therapy, they were resistant to working with his current teacher at the Tutoring Center and his teacher at the Charter School. The ABA company wanted to continue a few more months although the insurance did not want to approve additional days based on his progress and goals met. I decided that the ABA company was not a good fit and he started at the Tutoring Center full time.

After the school year ended, I enrolled Mahalek in the summer program at the Tutoring center to help keep him afloat academically and give him a chance to transition in without the demands of schoolwork for the academic year. The plan was to keep him enrolled in the Charter School for second grade. He would also attend the Tutoring Center to assist me with his schoolwork and interaction with his peers. This was a huge relief for Mahalek and me. For the first time in years, we were able to come home some days and just spend time together. He still had his tough days that resulted in him disrupting and destroying areas of the classroom. I tried my best to reach out to others to help me address these behaviors at school, not only to maintain a balance, but also so it wouldn't be reinforced that I would show up every time he had a meltdown. The teacher at the Tutoring Center began to help with reaching out to others when Mahalek had tough days. Initially, it worked out well and then it slowly phased out. There was less and less willingness to help with addressing behaviors. As I was getting more and more exhausted and feeling like I was running out of options, the people I was reaching out to for help seemed more intolerant of the same story and circumstances Mahalek got himself into. Thankfully, I had quite a bit of leave saved up at that time and began to take mental health days to rest and be present if Mahalek had a tough day. I tried my best to use the resources I had that were present for Mahalek, so I balanced my mental and emotional wellbeing, while responding to him reasonably.

I was very focused on working through my past traumas and healing my wounds so I could be better for me and Mahalek. I wanted him to see me doing the work just as I expected him to do.

Along my healing journey, I became more grounded and aware of who needed to be in my circle and who did not fit anymore. I needed people who understood or were open to understanding where I was to help me stay in a positive place. I began to see that Mahalek's behaviors were sometimes exacerbated by my inability to stay level. When I got worked up, anxious, or upset, so did he. This made me really focus on my emotional control and vulnerability so I would be able to be that sounding board for him. As I began to heal from the past traumas, with the help of the right support, I began responding to Mahalek from a more positive and balanced place. Little did I know this would make him more receptive to me and he began to trust me more, following my lead while learning how to navigate those tough emotions.

During my personal shift and the new people I had in my life to support me, Mahalek struggled with the thought of me spending time with others or taking phone calls and sometimes he acted out to get my attention. I really had to be intentional about my self-care and setting boundaries even with Mahalek. Setting boundaries with Mahalek was a bit rocky for about a year. The boundaries I was setting with Mahalek included establishing a time that we would spend together at home and when I would interact or talk with others on the phone to help ease his anxiety. On the other hand, I had to establish the boundary of him allowing me private time to spend in my room for a moment like he did in his room. He often felt like I didn't want him when I set boundaries with him. I wanted him to learn how to respect my personal boundaries like he had to do for others in social settings and embrace his solitude to help with emotional regulation. I looked for other events or things he could participate in, for interaction with others outside of myself, so he could build those relationships and feel like he could spend time with other people outside of me.

I decided it was time to start Mahalek in some type of extracurricular activity to help him learn how to work with others, serve as an outlet, and have coach mentors. He was resistant to my efforts of placing him in basketball, he didn't want to resume music lessons that were paused during the pandemic and was not receptive to the few martial art practices I took him to. To figure out what he may be interested in I began YouTubing boys his age who were playing sports based on what was offered at our local YMCA. When I showed him a video of children playing soccer, he immediately expressed an interest. I decided to enroll him for the spring at the YMCA. He was excited to go, but nervous as to what to do. He enjoyed soccer and the interaction with the children on his team. It took him a little bit of time to understand the flow of practice and gain confidence in his abilities.

When his games began, he was excited and engaged. However, when the rules came into play, and he had to take turns, he became a little defiant. He didn't understand how to play in a team format and was just nervous about the game in general. Mahalek had issues with taking turns, picking up on social cues, and understanding that the things he experienced were temporary. There were times when Mahalek just refused to play. I remember him being the goalie and he walked to the sideline, looked at me, started to cry and attempted to walk off the field. Often, he did things like this when he made a mistake or didn't perform the way he thought he should. I tried to have the conversation with him that it was okay, to try again, and have fun, but once he got to that point of frustration there wasn't much I could do to bring him out of that space besides taking him home. There were several times I just had to pick him up and carry him to the car. I was just as frustrated as he was, with his own defiance, because I typically was the one trying to help him through and calm him afterwards. It was just another thing that sometimes sent me into an unbalanced state.

Since Mahalek loved playing soccer, I started to use it as an incentive to encourage positive behaviors in school such as compliance with schoolwork, sharing with peers, and following the teachers' instructions. Once his teachers caught wind of him playing soccer and that it was used as positive reinforcement, they reinforced this concept in school settings as well. There were times that his behavior was so bad I had him skip soccer games until he straightened up. For instance, he got upset at school and didn't want to follow the teacher's rules and began hitting the other kids and destroyed the classroom. When I came from work to pick him up, I had to spend additional time helping him clean up the classroom and discussing the incident with his teacher. I thought having him skip a game would help him try to regulate his emotions, which it did the first few times. Then, as the behaviors became more unpredictable, skipping soccer games or attending soccer games wasn't much of an incentive anymore. Mahalek didn't seem to mind skipping games and I noticed that when he skipped them, he had all this energy that he could have let out during the game. He began to associate soccer as a punishment compared to the fun activity it was supposed to be. So, I decided to not skip soccer games or practices when he had tough days and looked for other ways to handle them. Mahalek played soccer for a few more seasons and then he began to lose interest in the sport when he was eventually introduced to flag football.

As he finished the summer program at the Tutoring Center and began to start the second grade, the Tutoring Center location changed to accommodate the growing numbers of students who attended. All the students had a little trouble with the transition, so the teacher was very tolerant of Mahalek's difficulties. He often asked to go back to the old location just because it was familiar. I remember with the transition he was more aware of who was dropped off when he could see the cars in the parking lot. This made him a little frustrated when he saw other kids arriving before him. He was very mindful of the time and if he arrived late, despite my reassurance that school hadn't started yet, it increased his risk of having a tough day. I started to take him to school a few minutes earlier so he could have a little play time as the other students came in and then he transitioned into the program for the day. The transition to the new location had its ups and downs and he started to embrace the change.

Chapter 8: What I Learned with Homeschooling, Pandemic and Resources Used

What I Learned With Homeschooling and the Pandemic

I learned the importance of self-care and what that included. My mental and emotional wellbeing depended on it and so did Mahalek. As a child I grew up in a household with poor boundaries and emotional instability. My response to past traumas turned me into a people pleaser with poor boundaries to try to keep the peace and not upset anyone. As I became an adult and did way too much for people without setting boundaries, while neglecting myself in the process, it kept me in an overloaded state. Sometimes I responded to Mahalek from a huge deficit because I didn't have anything left to give, and I couldn't be what I needed for him. The divorce and me revisiting my childhood wounds made me more committed to caring for myself. There was a point in time, when Mahalek was younger, that I became suicidal because I felt like there was no way out of feeling so overwhelmed when I had the inability to set boundaries and say "no". The thing that brought me out of that thinking was where Mahalek would be if I wasn't here anymore. I decided to get myself in order and began a path of healing to save me for him. I didn't want to give up even though things were hard. I felt so alone and unsupported, but when I looked at him, I knew I had to dig deep to get to a healthier place. As I healed, I began to teach Mahalek ways to practice self-care for himself. Although I had a lot on my plate, I wanted to work from a balanced healthy place versus the unhealthy balance I had experienced before.

I began to learn new ways to care for myself. Exercise and running were always my self-care activities. Occasionally I was a bit excessive with it, when I was overwhelmed and was physically exhausted, which sometimes made me feel sick. I began to practice meditation with yoga and that helped me refocus. The three biggest things I started to do were reading, journaling, and listening to podcasts. A good self-help book was recommended that helped me stay in the present. I was so depressed in the past and what led to my present situation I had to be very intentional about staying in the present. This led me to read self-help books about not only how to continue to heal, but how to be a healthy woman and mother for Mahalek. I didn't want my past traumas to impact my ability to connect with Mahalek. Journaling was my outlet to express my thoughts and feelings while podcasts helped me stay motivated along my healing journey. Another thing that I continued was therapy. Mahalek and I stayed in therapy and eventually started family therapy.

I learned that I had selected people in my life previously that I thought were safe. I realized that those same people tended to be unavailable emotionally and most likely were selected due to my inability to fully express my emotions. I was very transparent and outspoken about how I was feeling with people I trusted when I didn't always get that same openness back in return. I realized that I needed to have connections with people who could also be empathetic and have the capacity to understand my perspective. More so I wanted to be heard and understood. I also wanted to make sure I was able to hear and understand others in return. While dealing with Mahalek's complexities with autism I found it very difficult to fully express how I felt to people and didn't feel completely understood. It made me feel alone, isolated, and sometimes led to frustration from my unrealistic expectations. When I learned how to choose those who had the capacity to understand me and what I was dealing with, my life began to go in a positive direction. This gave me a better foundation to be the support Mahalek needed.

What Resources Were Used to Get Through Homeschool and the Pandemic?

I went against cultural stigmas and family perceptions and decided to go to therapy. It was suggested to me through the years and I just dismissed it. I had been told and advised growing up that as time passes, or with distractions, we can move past the pain. I found the only way to address it was to tackle it head on. Sure, this was something I needed to do for me. However, Mahalek motivated me to follow through and stick with it. How was I supposed to teach him how to be healthy and regulate his emotions if I didn't do the work to do the same? The initial part of therapy was so painful and draining because it exposed the past shame, guilt, and hurt. It did help me identify how I got to a place where I had very few boundaries. This was a big reason I was so overwhelmed. I'm such a giving person and I could not say no. This was one of the first lessons I learned in therapy was to say "no" and it was okay to set healthy boundaries, not only to protect my peace, but to also keep me in a balanced state. This was a process for me and something I reinforced with Mahalek.

I utilized the YMCAs for sports since they were flexible, allowed every child to have playing time, and the requirements as far as practices and games worked well with my schedule. The options the YMCA had for sports made it a little easier for me to allow Mahalek to try them with little pressure. I had grown up playing competitive sports and I knew firsthand how it could get out of hand. When I played sports as a child, I had the pressure to perform the best I could with the intent to achieve a scholarship to pay for college. I had a very hard time transitioning to college and not playing sports due to the pressure I felt, and my identity was wrapped up into it. Sports, specifically basketball, was an outlet for me to cope with a lot of the dysfunction I experienced growing up. This is not to say that Mahalek's experience would be the same as mine, especially early on. However, as I was becoming more aware of some of the childhood wounds and traumas I had I wanted to make sure I was not intentionally causing any for him and taking the fun out of it. I wanted him to enjoy the sports he participated in and fully enjoy his childhood.

I created a calming space at home for Mahalek like the calming room he went into at the sensory gym. Mahalek loved the calming space at the gym once he discovered it. After a few meltdowns in the gym where we had to go in there to help him calm down, he eventually found his way there if things became too much. That was one of the things I loved about the gym. When Mahalek had his meltdowns, it was truly a judge free zone, and I had a place that I could go to calm him that wasn't my car. There were things in the safe room such as dim lights, calming music, sensory toys, and a beanbag chair where we could lounge together and calm down. I decided to put a space together like the gym in our home. It was in a corner in his playroom sectioned off by curtains in the previous home and I adapted his new room to function dually as a bedroom and calming space. He went there often to calm down and I was in it quite a bit myself to help him relax. The nice things about the calming space were that it was in a separate area away from others in the home so he could express himself and take the time needed to work through his feelings.

Mahalek and my new start gave me the ability to choose a place that would be safe. This included allowing those with good intentions to enter our space. It was important for both of us to feel like we could fully let down, relax, and express ourselves in our new environment with no judgment. Sometimes this looked like limiting the number of visitors and sometimes it did not allow those who were not emotionally safe to enter our space. I needed the space to learn how to live for me and balance being a woman and mother. Mahalek needed the space to feel comfortable with low stimulation. For the most part, we have maintained a peaceful household that is full of love. Even when he has his meltdowns, here and there, it is a place where those behaviors can be addressed and he can quickly return to that comfortable environment. This is not to say the place where we lived prior to this was the worst, we just had less control over how the environment was managed. Also, my lack of boundaries contributed to that as well. As I learned healthy boundaries, I reinforced them as quickly as I could.

Chapter 9: The Escalation

Mahalek began to become more defiant as he progressed in the second grade. He began to seek attention from his destructive behaviors. He had become accustomed to people responding when he became upset. He also started to become a bit of a bully to get his way. He had this underlying anger that manifested in a very scary way. The thing that kept me on my toes was the fact that sometimes those behaviors came out of the blue, with no warning or pattern, which made it a bit harder to determine his triggers. I immediately had him meet with a therapist who specialized in childhood trauma. It was determined that he was acting out due to pain he was experiencing from a previous trauma which was most likely the divorce. The scary thing was sometimes he would seek out either women or children he knows couldn't fight back. This was hard for me to process because it reminded me of the abuse I had experienced, and I didn't want Mahalek to grow up and become like my abusers. I also didn't want Mahalek to become aggressive at home as he grew older because I knew I would have to exhaust other measures to keep our home a peaceful environment. I worked hard during this time to keep my past out of the way of how I responded to Mahalek. I was fearful that I would respond to him based on how I did with abusers in the past. Besides, my child was crying out for help, and I needed to figure out a way to be there for him.

Mahalek continued to have problems with separation anxiety. This turned into anger at home when he chose to ignore my boundaries set when I needed time to myself. I remember needing to take a nap and I told him I needed to lay down for a short amount of time and then I would be back out in the living room. At the time he wanted to watch TV with me in the living room, but I just needed to rest, and I was so exhausted from work. After I explained this to him and made sure he had activities to keep him occupied he decided that he wanted me to stay up with him and not take a nap. As I left the living room and walked to my bedroom, he followed me. When I closed the door, he started banging on the door and screaming. I tried my best to ignore him thinking he would stop since he did not like being ignored. After a while, I came back out to the living room to have a conversation with him since he wouldn't stop, and he just lost it. He began coming at me to hit me and started screaming. I had nothing left to give him at that point because I was already so exhausted. Every time Mahalek decided to challenge my authority and have a meltdown there wasn't anyone I could call who would come get him or even attempt to show up to give me a break. At that time, I managed to get someone on the phone to talk to him and calm him. He was able to verbalize that his reasoning for being upset was because he didn't want me to take a nap and wanted me to stay with him.

My boundaries extended to other areas at home as Mahalek went into the pre-pubescent stage. Mahalek is a very affectionate child and likes hugs. As a small child he liked to lay on women's legs and hug them. The older he got he had a hard time understanding how that behavior was inappropriate. For instance, when he was a small child, I used to lay in bed with him until he fell asleep or to read him a book and sometimes, he would attempt to lay on my stomach or leg versus a stuffed animal or pillow until I redirected him. As he grew older, I read a book to him while sitting on the side of the bed or we watched TV while sitting up in bed. He was in the process of learning how things changed the older he got and was learning what was appropriate and what wasn't. The thing I didn't realize at the time was that Mahalek was looking for affection from me even if it was a quick hug to help him emotionally regulate. Often, he thought if he didn't get a hug from me, I didn't love him, and I was rejecting. I struggled with why he felt like that and felt guilty for not showing him love the proper way or so I thought at the time. Only to find out while in therapy that Mahalek was looking for ways to validate my love for him since he felt invisible when he was ignored or perceived as a bad kid based on his past behaviors. He was beginning to feel like no one else cared about him and he lost confidence in himself, so he categorized himself as a bad kid. This only fueled his anxiety and aggressive behaviors when he was triggered.

    I started to reach out to everyone I could, and those I felt would be able to reach Mahalek in a different way than I could. I really believed he needed a male presence to help him learn how to emotionally regulate. I was doing the best I knew how to do as his mother. There were times where he met with male mentors that had talks with him about appropriate and inappropriate behaviors. During his interactions with them he was receptive, but his change in behaviors became short lived. Mahalek continued to become more resistant to schoolwork. Suddenly, the new schoolwork that was introduced was too hard or he told himself he couldn't do it without trying. I even met resistance at home when it came to that. At school he noticed it took him longer to complete his work while others had a little free time or moved on to the next task. This made him even more upset because they weren't going at his pace. Mahalek truly wanted things his way and wanted everyone to follow suit even though it didn't work that way. Thankfully his teachers were understanding of where he was and adapted his schoolwork based on his level. As he adjusted to them decreasing the load of schoolwork, he began to take advantage of this at the Tutoring Center and resisted more to get out of doing schoolwork even at his level. This led to him having more work that he needed to complete at home to stay caught up, which limited the free time he had at home. This was not something he was happy with nor was I. I was coming home after a long workday to help him with schoolwork and get him settled. Then I had more work to do and would still be catching up after midnight only to wake up and do it again.

 To help lighten everyone's loads a bit, and help his teacher out, there were a few things that were put into place. I reached out for additional help when there was a potential of him escalating and an on-call schedule of individuals who could come to the Tutoring Center to assist was developed. There were a few times the teacher called and those listed on the schedule appeared at the school. The first few times Mahalek was so surprised that someone other than me had arrived he calmed down a bit. After he got used to it, I still had to leave work to help de-escalate him or take him out of the environment altogether. I even took some days off and readjusted my schedule so I could be present in the Tutoring Center to see how he responded during instruction and intervene if he got upset. Mahalek was not too fond of me being present in the classroom and expressed that he felt embarrassed because no one else's parent was there. Mahalek continued to find loopholes in the methods placed. I had to get creative with realistic incentives that could be reinforced at the Tutoring Center. For example, I started a chart at home where he could earn money or a play date with a friend based on his behavior. At that time, he didn't have the greatest understanding of money or interest in earning it, so I changed to incentives such as small toys. In collaboration with the Tutoring Center, we decided to use extra play time during after school care with one of his friends as an incentive. There were activities I had planned for us to do at home after I picked him up that didn't involve schoolwork if he followed instructions and completed it at the Tutoring Center.

    We had to get creative in our ways to get him to complete schoolwork as well. With his main curriculum being online he had learned to go through the online curriculum to mark it as complete. Then when he had to complete supplemental work, such as worksheets, he got upset because it required him to put in real effort. Even though he knew how to do the work, he just didn't want to. Mahalek is a kinesthetic learner, and he learns best by putting his hands on it or writing things out. I printed all his worksheets off to give to the teacher at the Tutoring Center and she would make copies for some of his friends to work on the same worksheets with him to increase his compliance. This was very effective in getting him to complete things appropriately and I uploaded those sheets so he wouldn't have option to click through the information.

Mahalek had become used to the online curriculum reading instructions to him. Mahalek did not like reading in general and reading out loud made him nervous. Sometimes it led to a meltdown. Reading was a major trigger for him that caused a lot of anxiety. I worked hard with him every night with his reading. He needed to be able to independently read instructions for his benchmark tests since he wouldn't have the option of those being read to him at that time. His teacher at the Charter School began to give him activities to help prepare him for benchmark testing early. She did her best to test environments that would work for him to test accurately. One day we met at a library for Mahalek to take a few short tests in a private room. She was unsure of how well he would comply and wanted me present in case I needed to facilitate the process or address behaviors. He typically wasn't aggressive with her, since their interactions were mainly one on one, but he would run out of the room if he didn't want to complete something or was overwhelmed. During his testing, he took short breaks along the way to increase his compliance to get an accurate assessment. These academic adjustments and concerns had me think more about what accommodations he may need.

Mahalek was due for his follow up re-evaluation assessment, and I went ahead and included my concerns about his academic performance. I wanted it addressed during his re-evaluation assessment to help the teachers come up with a better plan of how to keep him on track academically. During his re-evaluation assessment, the psychologist stated that some scores may not be accurate due to his inattentiveness and refusal to do some of the activities. After his psych re-evaluation was completed and I received the results, I contacted the Special Education principal and Mahalek's teacher at the Charter School to update his IEP. I wanted both his academic accommodations and behavioral issues listed in addition to his current speech goals. This is when I was told that the behavioral items noted in the report, and seen during co-op or individual meetings with his teacher, wouldn't be included due to their limited ability to speak to those with him being in the virtual curriculum. On top of that the IEP wasn't something they had to do based on him being enrolled in the virtual portion. However, the IEP did get updated based on my request to include his new evaluation results and testing accommodations needed. In addition to including updated results and testing accommodations, they decreased some of the work Mahalek was assigned which helped him tremendously.

As things seemed to come together the best way they could at the time, I was battling the judgment of others as a newly single mother. Most people had no clue or even thought that I was married when I had Mahalek. I just didn't feel the need to explain or even mention my relationship status and I still ended up having to address it repeatedly with others. It was assumed that I had a child out of wedlock when I inquired about resources or stood my ground when advocating for him. I was treated like an inadequate mother until they found out I was divorced and it changed some people's perception of me. I was often seen as the angry Black woman, who just so happened to be educated and single, when I persisted with advocating for Mahalek. I remember going to a support group shortly after the divorce and immediately feeling like an outcast. These women talked about their struggles with special needs children and then quickly followed up with how their husband's helped in the process. When I voiced my frustrations of working multiple jobs, and feeling so overwhelmed when Mahalek was aggressive at school or social settings, it was followed by silence and blank stares. One mother broke the silence and verbalized how she struggled with something similar. The other women tried their best to offer solutions for me such as seeking support among family and friends. Once they found out I was divorced and doing my best with rebuilding a positive support system that was adequate for Mahalek, there was very little interaction or advice they had for me. Not only did I feel out of place with people who didn't identify with me, but I also felt that much more isolated with the additional stigmas people placed on me. That was the last time I attended the support group and have struggled to find one that works for me ever since.

We both were on the journey to learn how to emotionally express ourselves while dealing with stigmas and past traumas. Mahalek fell victim to the hurt and sadness he felt from what he perceived to be rejection from others, especially when he had rough days. This led to his behavior escalating even more during his meltdowns. His aggressive behavior and destruction of property had become worse. There were a few occasions where the police came to the Tutoring Center to talk to Mahalek and discuss the potential consequences of his behaviors. Sometimes the mention of his behavior or hearing how others perceived his meltdown sent him right back into another one. One day I was called by the teacher at the Tutoring Center because Mahalek was hitting the other children and had run out of the building. I quickly got myself together and headed toward the center which took about 40 minutes for me to arrive. In the process of collecting my things to head there, I was told by the teacher that she recommended I call 911 along the way for extra assistance. She was hesitant to call even though she needed help because she didn't want the police to come with force or place Mahalek in a less than ideal situation with the police. So I went ahead and made the call. The entire drive my stomach was so unsettled. I never thought I would ever be in a position where I had to call the police on my own child. All the scenarios I observed from other African American men in my life, or in the world, that ended badly were at the forefront of my mind. However, deep down I knew in that moment that choice was the best and safest option for Mahalek until I got there. When I arrived, the officer was there talking to him and calming him down. The officer was very good with him and didn't want to exert any force because he was so young. I was truly thankful for the officer being so understanding and mindful of the fact that if not handled carefully, this could add additional trauma. After he got settled, I knew that something had to be done differently.

 I was very resistant to placing Mahalek on any medication. I wanted to explore all options before that was even considered as an option. When he was attending the first ABA therapy center and the Director mentioned medications in the parent meeting, I became very frustrated and defensive. When I verbalized my refusal of placing him on medications, she proceeded to explain to me the difference between a psychologist and psychiatrist like I didn't know the difference, at least that's how I perceived it. At that moment all I heard, whether it was correct or not, was that my child was out of control, and they would rather deal with him in a medicated state, and I was unable to make sound medical decisions for him based on my lack of knowledge. That day I felt so defeated and his current situation had me reflect on that experience. I was worried about the side effects and didn't want him reliant on medications to control his emotions and behaviors. I wanted him to learn the proper coping strategies to stay in a healthy state. Despite my efforts, he continued to struggle with his aggression, and I became more open about putting him on medication to help manage it.

The day I had to call the police really changed my perspective about medications. I had begun to reflect on all the things I tried before. For instance, I used some essential oil blends to help him stay calm, which was more effective when he was younger. The older he got the less effective they became. I then shifted to cannabis oil and Chinese herbal blends recommended by his pediatrician. These helped somewhat. However, the cannabis oil was so hard to dose and to determine the effective dose I felt like it made him worse. I then proceeded to use magnesium oil and magnesium supplement gummies that did indeed help him relax. I would give him a few gummies before school and leave a few in his bag for his teacher to use around lunch time to keep him calm and focused on school. The magnesium gummies were very helpful, but over time they became less effective. When I noticed that the children who had been so tolerant of Mahalek's behaviors became more fearful, I decided to explore the medication route.

I was very nervous to begin the medication journey with Mahalek, but confident in my ability to manage it. I decided it was time to go to his pediatrician's office to express my concerns and openness to placing him on medication to keep himself and others safe. This was a difficult decision for the both of us and there was some concern about the medication side effects. However, I made it clear that all other options were exhausted, and this is something that was necessary to keep everyone safe. After discussing more of his history and increase of aggressive behaviors the decision was made to start him on Risperidone.

When Mahalek was prescribed Risperidone, I knew that it would take at least two to three weeks before we started to see some of the effects take place. I continued the incentive program at home to help manage his behaviors in the meantime. Then I decided to put together a one-page sheet of his behaviors and how to address them, then passed them out to his teachers and others who were interested and involved in his care. I figured the one-page sheet would be a quick reference for people to use to help prevent a meltdown or manage his triggers. I rearranged my work schedule so I could be closer in case he did have a tough day and no one else was able to get to the Tutoring Center in time. I began to accept the fact that although some individuals showed up to help when he escalated from time to time, they didn't know exactly how to address him in that state and sometimes felt uncomfortable intervening. I didn't want to put others in a position where they had to provide that space for him. I felt like that was my responsibility. At that time, I was willing to do whatever I needed.

Chapter 10: What I Learned About DeEscalation and Resources Used

What I Learned About De-Escalation

The more clarity I got as I worked on myself, it made it a little easier for me to identify Mahalek's triggers and respond in a timely manner. When he was smaller it was still too difficult to identify outside of the feeling I had because he couldn't really communicate things to me. I relied on his patterns and my intuition. The older he got the more he was able to use his words to express his feelings. I learned about more triggers outside of his difficulty with transitions and feelings of being overwhelmed such as people singing and dancing, arriving late to school, a change in routine which included the weather, and when he was sick or had breathing difficulties. I wasn't sure what the deal was with people and singing then because he loved listening to music in general. My thoughts were that it just was too much going on and he was taking in too many stimuli he wasn't prepared for. As he got older, he began to be more tolerant of singing and dancing. Sometimes at home or in the car he joined in with me. As far as arriving late, the anxiety he felt if he thought school started before he got there, or people were there before him caused me to change my routine. I had to either schedule appointments toward the end of the day or just not bring him to school altogether if he joined in later. Sometimes the days when I couldn't avoid the interruption, I let him bring a comfort item approved by the teacher. I also noticed that with weather changes, mainly the barometric pressure changes, and breathing issues it made his anxiety worse and gave him less ability to emotionally regulate. The thing he began to verbalize was that it made him nervous, and he didn't like people looking at him.

I learned how to offer appropriate incentives to reinforce positive behavior. I got better at adapting incentives as he got older and used other's feedback to help. Mahalek would work hard to complete school tasks and regulate his emotions for small pieces of candy, stickers, or stars. This helped keep him on track since he could see how his good behaviors were rewarded. On the other hand, if he didn't earn an incentive due to a bad behavior that sometimes resulted in him having a meltdown. Sometimes he would pull it together because he thought about the consequences he would have when he got home. He often expressed how upset he was with me when privileges, such as his pad or TV, were taken away. Mahalek had a hard time understanding that he could change his actions and earn trust. Sometimes he thought that once something happened there was no going back and he convinced himself he was a bad kid. Not only had he convinced himself he was bad, but also convinced himself that everyone else felt the same way, even if they said something different. I had him seeing a counselor at the time to help address some of his negative self-talk and social misunderstandings. I read positive affirmations daily, so I started to read them to him and speak about positive affirmations on the way to school and back home to shift his mindset. He struggled so much with his confidence and self-esteem at this time. I was very saddened to see it. I placed a lot of blame on myself and felt guilty for having to work so much and felt like I had failed him. I began to learn that Mahalek was at an age where he had to learn how to control himself. All I could do was guide him with the tools and he had to do the rest. This helped me give myself some grace in the process.

As his behaviors got worse and people got worn out with the same story of Mahalek acting out, I felt like my resources became even more limited. There was one day I melted down in my closet after Mahalek had an episode at the school. I just came home, got him settled and lost it. I was tired of everything being on my shoulders with really no one to turn to. I was also tired of the fact that when I did tell people they would express they understood and offered to help, but wouldn't really follow through with it. I started to blame myself for everything such as his behaviors, his diagnosis, the divorce, having to work so many jobs and the impact it had on Mahalek. This is when I learned to open my eyes to the few people who were there and lean on them. Asking for help was very difficult for me. I was a survivor and was always able to survive on my own no matter what. The emotional turmoil and stress that went into helping Mahalek balance, working on healing my wounds, and trying to stay positive was becoming harder to do on my own. I learned to be receptive to the few who were willing to help and were consistent in doing so. I was told that I needed to set my emotions to the side and look for what I was missing.

When I began to do that, I was able to process better and come up with solutions. On top of that, I really leaned into my spiritual faith to help me cope and stay on track.

What Resources I used to De-Escalate Him

I was embarrassed to admit when I had to call the police on Mahalek to help at the Tutoring Center. I drove that day with so much fear and anxiety and thought to myself, after all the things that have taken place with African American men and the police here, I'm resorting to them for my son. I was afraid of what I would see when I arrived. At the same time, I was getting to a place where I wanted my son to have some type of reality check so he would slow down and think about these behaviors instead of being so reactive. My gut was turning at the thought of things going bad and him ending up as a statistic. That day my perspective changed a bit of what the police could do to help him. The police station just so happened to be across from the Tutoring Center and often the teacher would have one of her friends from the station come over to speak to him. They were very good with him and helped reinforce what we were trying to get across to him. Although there were times when Mahalek thought it was a fun visit, because of his fascination with their profession and cars, at least it stopped his behaviors. If the behaviors continued, there was someone to help calm him down in a controlled way. I began to accept the fact that, if needed, in the future I would be okay with that. The underlying anxiety of him dealing with the police is still there. I discovered a program the police department had in my area where I could enroll Mahalek as a child with autism. If someone called on his behalf, it would flag him as a child with a disability, so they could adjust their approaches. This helped put me at ease and more open to the police being a much-needed resource.

I had watched how Mahalek interacted with the males at the Tutoring Center and how he always asked for the males in the family. He was coming into the stage where he was trying to figure out what he would look like when he grew up. Sometimes Mahalek would just tell me he was afraid to grow up and wanted to go back to when he was a baby. He was also looking for men who could show him how to stay balanced and hold himself accountable. Mahalek quickly realized that his behaviors scared the girls and women. He used that as a scare tactic to get what he wanted. It was recommended to place him in the Big Brothers Big Sister program so he could have a consistent mentor. I tried to get him set up at that time and had way too much on my plate and dropped the ball. However, as he got older, I finally followed through with starting that process. In the meantime, there were a few males that stepped up to talk to him and hang out with him on occasion for guidance. He listened and did well for a bit. Until he realized these men wouldn't be the people who showed up at the school or defended those in the classroom, then those efforts were short lived in minimizing the behaviors. I was very open to the male perspective and used the guidance that was given to me to help him.

Mahalek's behaviors toward women were attempted at home with me when he didn't get his way or wanted additional time with me despite the boundaries I had in place. Mahalek pushed my boundaries the more I responded to him from an emotionally stable place. My calm approaches began to throw him off so he escalated to get my attention and a rise out of me. For instance, sometimes I would go into my room to relax for a bit while he was in his. One day he just didn't want me to, since he couldn't see me, he lost it and started banging on my door. This was the same behavior I got any time I was on the phone, and he was around eight-years-old at the time. I used myself as the incentive. If he wanted to hang out with me, he had to respect my boundaries and use his coping strategies to get back into a calm state. I adjusted things to where I spent time with him at home, and our car drive was dedicated to him, in addition to some structured time at home. I started rewarding him with time he could spend with me and if he acted out, he would lose time with me. This took me almost a year to re-establish and get to the point where I could even attend a short meeting for work or phone call at home uninterrupted within reason. Even though I was his safe space, I felt that it was necessary for him to learn how to respect other boundaries including mine. Besides if I didn't set boundaries with him, there would be no pause from dealing with the things that arose from his behaviors.

Chapter II: Partial Hospitalization Program (PHP)

Mahalek went to the Tutoring Center one day and the call I received sent chills through my body. I was told that Mahalek had attempted to stab one of his good friends in the neck with a pencil, intentionally, and was still upset while I was on the phone with his teacher. That is the day that I knew he needed to be somewhere else to get him stabilized. I was fearful of what I would have to face with this child's parents when the news got out. Then I came to find out when I arrived, he had also started bullying some of the more delayed and nonverbal children because they weren't able to defend themselves. When the older kids went home for the day or were not present, based on their part-time schedule, he pushed boundaries with the younger kids. When I arrived, I put him in the car to calm him down and it took a long time. As I sat in that parking lot with him, and I saw the rage in him, I felt so helpless. I didn't even have it in me to call anyone. I was at a loss for words. I just sat with him and prayed. Something told me to get on social media and look around. I stumbled upon a post in a support group with a link to a Partial Hospitalization Program (PHP) that helps children with a similar diagnosis as Mahalek's, and aggressive behaviors, transition back into the public school system. While I was in the car with him, I searched for their information online and found a few locations near me and started to make calls. I was referred to contact the location that was close to my job. I won't forget the look on Mahalek's face when he knew I was calling around to find a different placement for him. He was terrified of change and what I had planned. In that moment, I knew it was time for him to go somewhere else for everyone's safety and to get the help he needed.

It took a few weeks to get Mahalek placed in the PHP. During the intake, which was scheduled within one week of me calling, it was determined that he qualified for the program, and we started the process quickly. While we were waiting for things to be finalized, his teacher at the Tutoring Center didn't feel the most comfortable with his return without some type of change. It was recommended Mahalek return in a week, after his recent medication adjustment. I agreed and made some adjustments to work virtually during that time until he was placed. Once he was placed, I immediately apologized in the Facebook group to all the parents with children attending the Tutoring Center and let them know that Mahalek was starting in a place to help stabilize him. I felt so bad about how Mahalek treated their children, and they were so understanding. They knew he wasn't trying to intentionally hurt anyone and was truly struggling with how to cope with everything. I was so thankful for their understanding, compassion, and support during the situation. To this day, when I bring Mahalek around to see them, they are so excited to see him and so are their children.

In the process of getting him started at PHP, I found a mother on the Facebook support group page who decided to message me about her experiences with her son at the PHP program who was a few years younger than Mahalek. She was very positive, but honest about how her son had a rocky start until he got used to it. I was preparing myself for things to get worse before they got better. I was so traumatized about being called every day to rush and pick Mahalek up that I just assumed it would be the same for the PHP. I remember the Director sitting down and explaining the process to me. I said I was open to being contacted, if needed, and I worked a few miles away. She let me know that they only contact the parent to update them, as needed, but not to pick up the child. This was to help the child understand that they had to follow the rules enforced without the parents, so when they went to public school, they wouldn't be expecting their parents to arrive when they had tough days. To say I was relieved was an understatement. The first day I dropped him off and didn't get a call I was so productive at work and at ease. I had lived with the anticipation of being called or having to leave as soon as possible constantly for the past five or six years.

After Mahalek got adjusted his core issues started to surface. The therapists, teachers, and psychiatrists at PHP quickly responded and developed a treatment plan for him. Although, I knew that I made the right decision about placing him at PHP, I received negative feedback about placing him there. It was sad to know that there were people in his circle who didn't fully understand the need or value of treating mental health issues. I quickly dismissed the negative perceptions and knew this was the best-case scenario for Mahalek to get the treatment he needed. I was so happy with the fact he got what he needed and was able to come home every day. He attended school with others in his grade level and the teachers within the school district came to the program in the morning to hold class while Mahalek went to group therapy in the afternoon. Some requirements for Mahalek's continued attendance was participating in individual therapy, group therapy, and weekly family therapy. The Psychiatrist visited him weekly and adjusted his meds based on his behaviors and reports from myself, the therapists, and teachers. Sure, the path was rocky, but in the end it was worth it. I was immediately relieved with him completing school during the school day with a teacher compared to me finding people to help or completing his schoolwork with virtual instruction. We were able to come home and focus on other things outside of schoolwork.

Therapy was pivotal for Mahalek, and he was so resistant at first. Group therapy was the most difficult for him. He struggled with understanding what his family dynamic was like in comparison to others. During group therapy, he didn't really understand the differences in family dynamics and didn't like having the attention on him. If he did speak, sometimes he would run out of the room. He had a male teacher and immediately gravitated to him. The teacher did his best reinforcing boundaries that were appropriate, so Mahalek would not only understand and respect them, but also still want to engage with him. For instance, Mahalek would try to sit in his lap when he got nervous and hug him at random times for comfort when he was trying to adjust. The teacher was very good about talking with him and explaining the importance of his boundaries along with what was appropriate and not. Mahalek developed a high level of respect for this teacher and started to model him. Mahalek thrived with consistency and the structured routine PHP maintained. Sometimes Mahalek challenged the female until he learned it wasn't going to be tolerated and he wasn't able to do the things we were able to do previously. While he adjusted, he would sometimes tell them he was going to act out to go back to the Tutoring Center to get me to come and get him. When he realized that wasn't going to happen, he became more defiant even with schoolwork after the start of the school year.

The demands of school brought about so much anxiety that Mahalek just came unglued or ran out of the classroom. He refused to do his schoolwork initially and really had to be walked along with one-on-one guidance. If not, he would either have a meltdown, run out of class, or sometimes try to run out of the building. Mahalek also struggled with peer interaction in the classroom and took what was delivered as sarcasm literally. Sometimes this infuriated him to no end. The first few months Mahalek was in a hold, sometimes up to ten times a day. The Psychiatrist tweaked his medications slowly each week. Mahalek started at PHP with one medication and ended up leaving with three routine medications and one medication as needed for extreme cases. He struggled most with the transition back to school after spending time with his dad's family. The therapists and I had to be creative with incentives to try to get him to comply each week.

Therapy was intense for Mahalek, and things got worse before they got better. I tried my best to be patient with him in the process as I reflected on my journey when I first started therapy. The triggers and the pain that is released when you are forced to process through everything can be very intense and seem to come all at once. Family therapy was one of the greatest things that we could have participated in. Although we had started it prior to working with PHP, it was more frequent and included things addressed in group and individual therapy which helped me understand the underlying cause of some of Mahalek's behaviors. Mahalek was very closed off at first because he was afraid of my reactions when he told the truth about how he felt or that he didn't know how he felt for that matter. I worked hard to maintain my cool when he expressed himself no matter how hard it was to hear. For some reason, I felt so much guilt for making some of the decisions I made to place us in a better position. Because of the changes it led to I blamed myself for everything and I thought Mahalek had blamed me too.

Therapy helped us work through those feelings and come to find out Mahalek didn't blame me at all. I learned more about what it meant to be his safe person and why he reacted to me the way he did. He felt like I was the person who accepted him, comforted him, and was the most consistent. At times it was still hard to determine where his pain was coming from. Later we realized part of it was his shame and lack of confidence in his abilities to keep his cool, interact appropriately with peers, and complete his schoolwork as things got more advanced. As he learned how to process his feelings he started to verbalize them to me. When I picked him up one day, he said to me, "mom I get nervous when people look at me and when the schoolwork is hard." I was literally in tears. This was one of the first times that I could recall him clearly expressing his feelings. It was also one of the first times I felt like I had done something right and maybe he would be okay.

As he became more open with his feelings and we both processed through everything, it gave me a little bit more clarity on what I could do to help him progress in PHP. The support I received at PHP gave me the ability to shift to other things I didn't have the time or capacity to address such as being more intentional about his diet and changing it. I had been told to monitor his diet as far as removing red and yellow dyes and foods with nitrates such as turkey lunchmeat and beef corn dogs. With all the moving pieces and his picky food preferences, some things I let slide until I got grounded enough to really make the shift. I had maintained a low carb diet and Mahalek was used to that for the most part. The hard part for him was removing foods with red and yellow dyes. Some of those foods that had those dyes were primarily his snacks he had at home and in the school setting such as Doritos. He would sometimes tell me if he just had a few he wouldn't act up. He was aware of why the foods were eliminated, but he still wanted to eat them in what he thought was moderation. After he got used to not having the foods with dyes, I remember him having chips with dye in them at PHP during lunch. I'm not sure if it was Doritos or Cheetos. He had the roughest few days after that at home. I used that experience to reinforce why he couldn't have those foods and how they contributed to his aggression.

Mahalek tested his boundaries more and more at PHP. When we had our sessions, he did not like hearing about what he had done or seeing what he had done in the middle of a meltdown. If

I was able to, I recorded him when he had a meltdown, or at least I tried the best I could, as I was helping him calm down. We watched the videos no matter how hard so we could talk about how he was feeling and what we could do differently. As he got into more holds from his attempts to get PHP to call me or just get out of going to PHP altogether, he turned to self-injuries. At first, I thought he was just hitting himself for attention like what he did as a young child. I quickly realized I was wrong. He was hitting himself because that was his way of punishing himself for not being calm enough, even during a meltdown, he added to the event by turning to himself for the shame of his behaviors. After he calmed down, he would express how he wasn't trying to hurt himself intentionally. He was so hard on himself, and it took months to get him out of the mindset that he wasn't a bad kid, he was just making bad decisions, but could make good ones. This was the hardest thing for me because it was the one thing I couldn't control. I couldn't control his thoughts or what he told himself. I kept at him with positive affirmations and made him say something positive about himself every day before and after school. As we got close to discharge, I remember him saying to me randomly "mom I am happy to be alive." The joy I felt with months of trying to get him to see himself in a positive light had paid off.

As Mahalek got more used to PHP he would have a few good weeks followed by a few setbacks. He was getting bigger and stronger, so it was taking more and more people to calm him and put him in a hold and the damage he caused was worse. To help him release some of that aggression, I ended up exploring other sports for him to play since soccer wasn't as interesting as it was for him previously. I found out he was interested in flag football, so I signed him up for it. He had so much excitement for the sport and the practices were so different from soccer, so it wore him out and made him calmer. There were times Mahalek struggled with making mistakes as he was learning the game, and his negative self-talk and self-doubt made it hard for him to want to try again. The second flag football practice he had; he ran a play based on what the coach instructed him to do. He made one mistake and he fell to the ground like it was the end of the world. The coach and his teammates tried to tell him it was okay and to try again, but Mahalek had checked out. I tried to get him to participate and try again, but he refused so I took him home for the day. I debated on just removing him from the team to save myself the trouble and to not compound his embarrassment. I apologized to the coach and briefly filled him in on what happened and how Mahalek felt. He told me that he understood but would like to see Mahalek at the game that was scheduled in a few days, so he learns that he can try again and develop his confidence. He told me his son, who was assisting him with coaching, had a similar feeling about the sport until he realized he was capable. To this day, I'm very thankful for the coaches' words because he convinced me to continue Mahalek in the sport. Eventually, he did develop that confidence and ended up loving the sport. Now I can't get him to play anything else but flag football!

There was a period at PHP that had become very rocky for Mahalek, even with ongoing therapy, diet changes, multiple medication changes, and his newfound love for flag football. Mahalek had a history of being in up to 50 holds per week. Over time that number decreased. However, there were times where he would just react and since he was getting bigger and stronger it was taking more people to put him in a hold. He began to become really upset during the hold because of the force it took to control him, and he started cursing at the therapists and sometimes spitting or blowing his nose on their clothing. One day I walked in to pick him up and they asked if I wanted to see if I could calm him down while he was in a hold, so I agreed to make the attempt. I walked into the room and asked him calmly what was going on and he immediately called me a "bitch." This was the first time he ever called me out of my name. It not only threw me off because I didn't curse at home, but it also made me so furious at the disrespect. After he calmed down he apologized, but to be honest, it took me a long time to get over that. He had to work hard to earn my trust again.

As he continued to struggle at PHP and the meltdowns intensified, he became more dangerous for himself and the other children. Part of it was his growth and the other part was him picking up on negative behaviors he saw the other kids do. I received a call from the therapist about them locking the building down and having the police come because Mahalek had become agitated and refused to calm down per their protocol and the amount of holds he had trended the past few weeks increased. This was the first time PHP called me to come and pick up Mahalek. He was enrolled there for about four months. I had to pick him up and take him to the emergency room (ER) with the police escorting us due to his behavior. They gave me the option to refuse, but warned me that child protective services may be notified, and I could be seen as negligent. I agreed to take him to the ER with the third-party statement they had written. Mahalek wasn't bothered by the visit at all and was refusing to communicate with the doctor once she was able to see him. He saw the visit as a break and an escape from the expectations at PHP. I remember waiting in the ER for over three hours to speak with the doctor to evaluate him. Mahalek was sent to the ER this time for just refusing to stop hitting others, trying to flee the building, and hitting the staff. Once the doctor in the ER spoke with him, she thought it was best for Mahalek to return to PHP since he wasn't there too long, and we were working on getting his medications adjusted. She didn't see him as a threat to others or himself based on his responses. The PHP staff felt bad for having to send him and his therapist checked on him throughout the stay at the ER and was looking forward to welcoming him back to PHP.

Mahalek straightened up for a few months after that ER visit. Then he went through a rough patch again and got upset at a peer in the classroom and had another bad meltdown. This time they tried their best to calm him down. He kept hitting himself and threatening to hit others. This was right after he had a few weeks of being in at least five holds a day. Based on his amount of holds, it was recommended I take him to the ER again for an inpatient evaluation. This time was an even longer wait of about eight hours to get him evaluated. I remember sitting at his bedside and continuing to catch up on my work and just trying to stay level. I must admit I was over dealing with Mahalek's behaviors and defiance. He looked at going to the ER as a treat because it got him out of school, and he didn't think it was that bad of a punishment. I can honestly say at that point I was ready for him to be admitted to inpatient so he could get the help he needed, learn his lesson, and give me a break. After his evaluation, the provider determined he wasn't a threat to himself or others. In addition to that, even if he was eligible for inpatient treatment, there were no beds available in the state at that time, so they discharged him, and he returned to PHP. When he returned to PHP and his psychiatrist followed up with him, he was prescribed Zyprexa as needed to calm him down when he got upset.

Mahalek continued to progress in PHP and was close to advancing to another level based on his short decrease in behaviors and increased compliance after the second ER visit. He was a little more open to doing his schoolwork and working with his peers. He verbalized having anxiety and fear about returning to the ER and going to inpatient. He was worried about not being able to come home and see his family. Then I got another call from PHP to pick him up immediately and take him back to the ER because he was attempting to stab one of classmates with a pair of scissors. Once I got there he was still upset, they tried to give him the Zyprexa and he would spit it out. I was told they got him to calm down for a short period and then he escalated again. He went back a few more times to attempt stabbing her. This time he was upset because his classmate used him as an example to a scenario in class. He viewed it as being sarcastic, not in context, and he didn't like it. After he calmed down a bit and we talked about it, he didn't understand how her actions were appropriate and weren't mean. I remember waiting in the ER for hours again. This time after he was evaluated, they informed me that they were going to admit him and were in the process of looking for placement. During that time, I had to remain present with him until they found a bed. I was very overwhelmed with so many emotions about him getting placed and I did my best to keep it together. After talking things though with a close friend, I realized that inpatient treatment was the best place for him, and I was ready. He pushed every boundary while in the ER thinking he was going home that day. I had to notify the police in the ER to help with his compliance. When a bed was found, the facility contacted me to let me know they were sending transportation and I had to follow them to complete the admission process. When the van arrived to take him to the local inpatient facility, he was excited to leave. He was so oblivious to what that admission would entail, I still have the video of him playing and laughing in the lobby.

Chapter 12: What I Learned During PHP and Resources Used

What I learned From His Time in PHP

I was hesitant to placing Mahalek in any type of mental health facility. Mainly because of the resistance I faced from family perceptions and some of the things I've seen as a nurse. I had to come to terms with the fact that Mahalek needed specialized mental health care for him to have a chance of being a productive citizen and improve those negative behaviors. I wanted him to have early intervention and avoid a criminal record when he got older. I had many connections with nurses, with various expertise, so I called around and spoke to a few about my situation and pending decision to follow through with placing him in PHP. It was confirmed that I was making the right decision to give him the best chance of improving his behavior. Some of the people I spoke with even shared stories with me about how they had to go down a similar road with their own children. This helped give me even more courage to follow through with the decision to place him in PHP to get him the help he needed. During this process, I learned that mental health programs have a lot of benefits and early treatment can change the trajectory of an individual. If I had delayed Mahalek's treatment or been resistant to it, I wouldn't have been able to get him as far along as he is today. I learned that placing him in PHP was the best thing for him and me to be able to have that support to work through the core of his behaviors so he could function better in the future.

Mahalek's aggression came on so quickly, and suddenly at times, that it made it difficult to identify his triggers. When he was younger, even though he couldn't communicate with them as well, with the help of ABA we were able to identify some of his core triggers to prepare for them. However, as he aged and with the divorce, it was a little bit more difficult for him to process all the emotions he had going on and he became so reactive. The focus for a while was to just keep him calm enough so he was safe, and safe for others, which overshadowed the investigation into his triggers. I learned the strategies that worked early on weren't as effective based on his new feelings and triggers. As he got older, his triggers evolved and manifested in a different way. I learned the true power of therapy and how it contributed to Mahalek expressing his real feelings that led to his triggers. For instance, in group therapy Mahalek was triggered often and would frequently flee the room or refuse to go altogether. As he got near the end of his program, he remained present because he had worked through his feelings of being nervous when others looked at him and his feelings about his new family dynamic. He was triggered in a group with the other children who talked about stepparents. Most children there had parents who were divorced or single, so Mahalek was trying to figure out how he related to the others.

Once he realized his family dynamic was like the other children, and that there wasn't anything wrong with it, he began to relax. He did well in individualized therapy and opened for the most part unless it was about the male presence in his life. This usually caused him to become frustrated. It took a while to learn he didn't want to express these concerns to me because he was afraid of my reaction. Once he learned that I wasn't going to react as he thought he began opening more and we were able to determine other ways for him to express himself.

One of my greatest fears was Mahalek becoming a statistic. As he got older, I couldn't help but feel overwhelmed with the thought of the world seeing him as threat if he wasn't able to get in control of his emotions. I don't want him to be seen as an emotionally unstable African American male that is perceived as a criminal and put in jail without the proper treatment or killed for that matter. I don't want him to suffer consequences that he can't bounce back from or make it more difficult for him to pursue what he's passionate about. The thought of losing him to the system or to violence kept me up at night and contributed to my anxiety. I learned that sticking with the proper treatment and addressing his behaviors early on gave him the best chance to have the tools to be a stable productive male. Mahalek has such a loving soul, so I know he is capable of achieving his goals. As he progressed in PHP, as difficult as it was, when I look back on the trends and how far he has come, I have faith he will continue to improve. It has renewed my motivation to stay steadfast to the course no matter how bumpy the ride gets.

What Resources I Used With His Time in PHP

I became more structured with my routine at home and kept it in line with PHP. Sometimes when Mahalek spent time in other places, that were not as structured, he came back worse until he got back to his routine. This was around the time that instead of fighting to maintain consistency in areas I wasn't present in I focused on what I could control. I made it very clear to Mahalek that even though he may go other places that didn't maintain a routine such as mine he was to follow the routine in place or accept the consequences such as losing privileges. He revealed to me how much he loved watching TV so losing TV privileges is where I started with consequences. For instance, on Mondays if he didn't follow the routine as planned and had trouble controlling his emotions, he lost TV time. He would lose privileges for a few days at a time depending on what he did. Then I posted a calendar in his room, so he knew what to expect. He knew when to take his medications, when to feed the dog, when to take out the trash, and when it was time to shower and go to bed. There was even time built in the schedule to finish schoolwork or read. After he got accustomed to the calendar, I just had to send gentle reminders for him to reference it and he just followed it. It made it much easier for him to adjust back into the environment.

I began to take others advice and prioritized time to myself. I was working so hard to make sure I did everything I could to help Mahalek. I was working three jobs with my full-time role in a leadership position, and I was running myself ragged. I was told by so many people including Mahalek's therapist that I needed to find a way to take time for myself. I had often found myself close to losing leave by the end of the fiscal year with my full-time position because I didn't take much of it, so I started utilizing my time off. Sometimes it started with me taking time off to just rest and take a nap. I was always either working, determining how I was going to address Mahalek's behaviors, or looking into resources for him so I had a hard time turning my brain off. This impacted my ability to sleep at night and it left me feeling so exhausted. Sometimes I would find myself sleeping hours on end when Mahalek was with his dad over the weekend. If I felt rested sometimes, I would just treat myself to breakfast or lunch. I enjoyed the uninterrupted time to just clear my head and treat myself. As much as I worked sometimes, I still had that survival mode mindset. I would do what I needed to do for Mahalek and neglect myself. So just taking myself out for a quiet meal, that I didn't have to make, was so nice and refreshing.

    I learned how to develop a variety of tools with incentives that were appropriate to use at home that aligned with PHP expectations. The therapists asked my input about what tools I used at home, to help them determine what to reinforce, and what I was doing to help take some things off my plate. During our therapy sessions, I had often spoken about some of the incentives I offered Mahalek, depending on his behavior, as well as the consequences. I started expanding on the resources I had created and written for him at home and passed those along to help decrease his behaviors at PHP. For instance, one incentive I started to use was letting Mahalek pick where he wanted to eat at the end of the week if got through the week with no holds. Since he had so many holds in the past, I wanted to help decrease that number so he was more confident that he could stay balanced and to give the staff a break. I was trying to remain hopeful that he could regulate better. When he had tough days, sometimes he had a harder time pulling it together if he thought the incentive couldn't be earned. So, we adjusted that if Mahalek used his coping skills to regulate the rest of the day, he could still earn an incentive. For example, even if he didn't earn the lunch with me after a tough day, but he pulled it together, he got an incentive from PHP. When Mahalek found out we were all on the same page, and if he used his coping strategies effectively he could still earn rewards, it became more effective. Over time, his incentives were given based on him going longer amounts of time with fewer holds and the ability to use coping strategies to help prepare him for discharge.

Chapter 13: Inpatient Admission

Admitting Mahalek to an inpatient mental health facility was hard to do and it hurt my heart to even go through with the admission process. A small part of me was anxious about what others would think of him being there and what support I would have as he stayed there. I started to reflect on all the times I showed up and dealt with his behavior alone. At that point, if those other people didn't support my decision, I didn't care. I had to do what was best for him while I was still making a living for us both. This was the best-case scenario at the time. The intake process was around 9 p.m. and I let PHP know that he was getting admitted so they could communicate that with his school. As the nurse collected his information and asked me questions, Mahalek told the nurse that I was a nurse as well. This was something I didn't typically tell nursing staff because I didn't want them to treat me differently. I was in a mental fog at that point and my nursing knowledge wasn't something I was able to discuss. After the intake was completed, the nurse told Mahalek to give me a hug, since he wouldn't see me for a while, and they took him back to his assigned area. As I walked out of the facility to my car, my heart dropped. It was dark. I just sat in the car and cried. Then I pulled myself together and went home. At least I knew he was getting the help he needed and he was safe. I used that time focusing on self-care and getting caught up with work. Outside of the occasional phone call, updating me about Mahalek's status, I stayed on track at work and was more efficient. I tried to get as much as I could done with him gone and lean on the support I had. I realized what all of the anticipation about having to pick him up in an instant had started to do to my mental health.

Mahalek stayed inpatient for five weeks. I struggled the whole time with him being gone. I was relieved that I was able to get things done, without having to monitor his behaviors, but I still missed him terribly. I would come home to face a place of silence and it was awkward. I found myself randomly going into his room as if he was still there. After the first week, I was able to go up for family therapy and to take him a few of his clothes. I could see in his face that he realized this was not where he wanted to be, and he would not be saved from the situation he got himself in. During his therapy session he just laid on me and hugged me the whole time. I knew he missed home and he was missed. However, I needed him to understand that he had to straighten up or he was going to have a rocky path full of consequences he wouldn't like. The doctor reviewed the plan with me and stated Mahalek would most likely be in the acute care side for five days and then moved to residential until he was stable. She anticipated no more than a two week stay at that time. I remained optimistic and hopeful that his stay would lead to some changed behaviors. After he was in for two weeks and he was close to his projected discharge date, he showed his true colors and had his first meltdown. I wasn't surprised it took that amount of time. Mahalek was good at being on his best behavior to get what he wanted until he didn't and then those reactive behaviors surfaced. During the first two weeks he called on a regular basis. He was only able to make one phone call, so he alternated between his father and me. However, after those first few weeks, when he realized his discharge was dependent on his behaviors, he didn't call home as much. He expected someone to save him and was upset because it didn't work out as he hoped.

The next three weeks during his inpatient stay were rough for him, and for me, to say the least. He made his stay so much worse by rebelling at every chance he got. He was in the pattern of thinking if he just acted up more, or said things that were inappropriate, his mom would come and get him. Although it was reinforced to him multiple times that he had to straighten up to come home, sometimes he would just hang up or not call altogether because he didn't get the response he wanted. He started rebelling at night by waking up and trying to hit the other kids and staff. The staff began to contact the doctor and they began changing his medications to see if he would calm down a bit. I became frustrated with the rapid change in his medications and the fact that they didn't resume his home medications as I reported. At the same time I understood the intent of the change, especially when he started to get more aggressive and violent to himself and others. I was called to consent to all new medications, which I approved, in addition to addressing any concerns I had about his home medications not being resumed and tapered off appropriately. I was willing to do what needed to be done to get him stabilized. One medication that was used routinely was Zyprexa. This was a medication that PHP had recently prescribed as needed when he started to become upset but since he was not able to regulate inpatient it became a routine medication. His behavior continued to get worse. They had no choice but to start giving him injections in his buttocks to get him to calm down. He would get upset over things such as having to get up when they asked or getting upset at a peer.

Around the end of week three, I started getting calls, almost daily, about him needing an injection and the holds he was placed in. He was sometimes injected and placed in hold up to three times each day. Some days were better than others. This was all because he was ready to go home. My heart was broken knowing he was so distressed. I kept myself occupied with work and self-care the best I could. I truly tried to embrace the time I had to myself, while he was an inpatient, but it was so difficult. I remember going to a holiday party for work and on the way I received a call to inform me that Mahalek needed additional treatment. He was going to be transferred to another residential treatment center where he may stay for up to three or four months. After I was off the phone with them, I arrived at the party and the residential treatment center called me to collect intake information for him. I was so sad at the thought of my son being away for so long for treatment, even though I knew this was what he needed. Making those tough decisions took a toll on me. As much as I tried to enjoy the party, I was very distant and disconnected. I couldn't stop thinking about what would happen next and how I would stay emotionally regulated.

When he got to the four week mark, I was told he didn't qualify for the services at the residential treatment center they had originally planned for him because he was so aggressive and unstable. Mahalek was still in the inpatient acute care unit which had an average stay of one week to get the children stabilized. Mahalek ended up staying on that unit the entire five weeks because he just kept getting worse. Then finally at the end of five weeks, I got a call that he was getting discharged because they had done all they could to stabilize him. All that to say he was so unstable and defiant, they just sent him home. I didn't know what to do besides remain faithful that he had learned from this experience, and he would do better going forward. Part of me knew, deep down, I had to be prepared to make harder decisions at home, if necessary. It was necessary for him to understand that his actions can get him into serious trouble in hopes that he would choose to make better decisions.

 When I picked Mahalek up from the inpatient facility he was so excited to see me, and I was surprised at how different he looked in just over one month of his admission. They had informed me over the phone, but I was still shocked at what he looked like. He looked like he had been in a fight and his mouth was busted in the process. I noticed he had a sore mouth and cracked lips. As I received the discharge instructions, he just sat there patiently until it was time to go home. I was in the process of teaching a three-day course, so I got him home that night to get him cleaned up and he spent the next few days with his father until I finished the course. When Mahalek returned home, he looked around like it was a strange environment. He had become so used to the surroundings and structure as an inpatient it took him a while to adjust to being back home. I kept him in a similar routine to help with the transition. Luckily his discharge date was around the holiday time, so school was out for the winter break and his program at PHP that he returned to was abbreviated.

After a few days of being home, he began to test my boundaries and I knew he was willing to take it as far as he did as an inpatient. I went to Walmart to do a little shopping and get some clothing for the upcoming cold months. We were in the clothing section looking for holiday themed pajamas for him to wear at PHP for the holiday pajama day they had coming up. Since it was so close to the holiday, I couldn't find anything in his size. He was so fixated on finding something to wear. When I let him know we had to go somewhere else he started tapping me on my arms to let me know he was upset. I ignored it initially since that was his way of trying to get my attention so I would react to him. However, the more I ignored him the worse he got. He went from tapping my arm to punching my arm and screaming in the store. He had just turned nine-years old at this point. I looked at him and spoke to him sternly. I let him know I wasn't tolerating the disrespect or him putting his hands on me. He continued to get more enraged in a way I've never seen him get, especially with me. Since we were in a public place I just checked out and got him out of there as fast as I could to avoid making a bigger scene than he had started.

I knew with that incident it was only the beginning of more to come. Besides, Mahalek was very smart and he was willing to do whatever he could to get his way. He often made the statement, "I couldn't have it my way," when we discussed his behaviors after a meltdown. The next day after visiting Walmart we were at home and he didn't like me telling him what to do. I was asking him to clean up and he just didn't want to. Once I reinforced his need to do the chores, I asked him to do it firmly. This made him upset.

My consequence for him not wanting to do chores was taking away a stuffed animal until the chore was completed. He got so upset, he started hitting me and throwing things around in the living room. The firmer I got, the more frustrated he got, and the destruction became worse. This was the first time the police came to our home because of his behavior. I won't ever forget the rage he had. I didn't even recognize him. I really thought it was because he blamed me for his inpatient admission. He was so beside himself during this time I kept people away because his behaviors were so unpredictable.

When the police came to our house to help get him under control, Mahalek was somewhat calm and spoke to the officers appropriately. He was surprised they were there, and I thought to myself as soon as they left, he was going to go right back into it. Then suddenly Mahalek started resisting the officers, screaming, and running through the living room and kitchen throwing things. By this time there were two officers who were present, and they placed him in a hold position in the middle of the floor. He was fighting and kicking in the hold, for what seemed like forever, but was only about ten minutes. Then I remembered I had those Zyprexa tablets that I could place under his tongue to get him to calm down. So, I gave it to him with the officer's present. He didn't like it and tried to spit it out. Within the next twenty minutes there was a third officer who arrived and was trained to address behaviors with special needs children. He tried his best to talk and reason with Mahalek, but Mahalek just got worse. He went from squirming on the floor in a hold to a hold on the couch. It took about an hour for him to calm down. He finally fell asleep once I gave him a stuffed animal to help comfort him. The officers called the crisis line during his episode, and they arrived about fifteen minutes after Mahalek had fallen asleep. Once the crisis staff arrived the officers left. The behavioral therapist with the crisis line talked with me and gave me a few resources. They didn't want to disturb Mahalek since he had just fallen asleep. I was exhausted mentally and emotionally at that point. When everyone left, I just disconnected from everything and wasn't in a space to talk with anyone.

Some of the things I noticed as Mahalek was becoming more acclimated at home was that his quick shifts in medication while being an inpatient had disrupted his mood and led to rebound aggression. This was something I became more aware of when he resumed his stay at PHP and the psychiatrist began trying to adjust his medications back based on his discharge paperwork. The abrupt discontinuance of some of the medications during his inpatient admission had caused him to have a bit of rebound aggression. This explained why he was more enraged and had a hard time calming down. I was under the impression that since he was an inpatient for so long, he would adjust to the changes. However, he was given so many medications just to calm down, it was hard to determine the effectiveness and the adverse effects. His psychiatrist at PHP was so understanding and adjusted his medications weekly to help him get back to baseline. Once his medications were balanced, there was huge change in Mahalek's behaviors. During this time, he was placed on Abilify which was more effective for him since his labs returned to normal after discontinuing Risperidone. He was stressed as an inpatient and adjusting back, those mouth sores continued. It took me a few weeks to get his mouth sores under control and healed. He didn't want to eat much because his mouth sores were painful and his lips were so bloody. He had fought with the staff during his inpatient admission, and then worked himself up so much when he returned home, that he was literally knocking his immune system down and developing mouth sores. When I brought this to his attention, he tried to act a little better so his mouth wouldn't be in as much pain. Luckily his PHP program was virtual during this time, due to the weather, and it helped decrease his anxiety of what others would say about his appearance.

Mahalek began to go back into the school year that January and was excited to see his friends at PHP. Once his medication regimen was worked out, and he adjusted to the routine reinforced at home, his behavior improved significantly. Around March, we began discussions of his transition to public school for the upcoming school year since he made such vast improvements. Mahalek's holds had significantly decreased to a few a month. He had become more compliant in school and was asking for help instead of fleeing from the classroom. He was even able to be the class leader and help others with their schoolwork if he continued to follow rules and stay regulated. He did not want to go back to the inpatient facility or to a different facility, for an even longer time, and started to verbalize this. The police and PHP had reinforced this concept if he decided to continue with his previous behaviors. I noticed Mahalek's anxiety increased when the discussion came up for him to transition. He had a slight increase in holds and some defiant behaviors. When this behavior was addressed in family therapy, he began to express that he was nervous about the transition since he was one level away. PHP tried to ease him into the last level of the program to prepare him for the transition, but he couldn't handle the mention of it. I finally concluded that his anxiety was so bad knowing about the transition that his transition had to come as a surprise to help him with compliance.

Over the next few weeks, PHP avoided the conversation and monitored his behaviors. During that time, Mahalek's conversations shifted about possible bullies at school. I tried my best to redirect and reassure him that bullies shouldn't be something he was concerned about. That didn't stop his persistence with talking about it constantly. One day I shared a story with him about how I was bullied around his age and how I ended up changing classrooms because of my discomfort. I didn't feel comfortable expressing myself until I was an adult. He found some relief in that. I guess he realized once again that he wasn't the only one experiencing similar feelings. I told him how I had to transition to a different school and state around his age, how I felt as a child when I moved from Los Angeles, CA to Del City, OK and what troubles I had adjusting. This was one of the first times I really got into discussions about my feelings at that time. This helped him to open to what he was truly afraid of. He was worried about being accepted and the perceptions of others if he did have a rough day. He thought he would be bullied and have no friends as a result. We began to shift our conversations to what behaviors he needed to show and coping strategies he needed to use to avoid those perceptions. That worked well until one day he went to PHP and realized he had moved up a level.

Mahalek was excited about moving up a level because he got more freedom. He was surprised because it was without warning, to eliminate his sabotaging actions, and his anxiety began to creep back in. He got into the car after I picked him up one day telling me about how he got lucky lunch because he moved to a new level. Lucky lunch was something he got at the end of the week if he didn't have any holds and behaved appropriately. He was so excited about it. There were weeks that he had one rough day that didn't result in a hold, but prevented him from getting a lucky lunch, and he began to handle it well. The few days it didn't go so well were when we had conversations about discharge. He started to fall back into self-sabotaging behaviors because he was afraid of going to public school. During our rides to PHP, I had him tell me one thing he was grateful for and one thing that was positive about going to school. He really struggled with this at first. His typical response was I don't know, which he found out was not a good enough answer for me. I often told him if you don't know that means we have more work to do. This usually made him dig deep and think a little harder to come up with an answer. It took about a month for him to start to speak positively about school, even though afterwards he still made it a point to let me know he was nervous. Some things he ended up saying was that he was excited to make new friends, he was a good kid, and he was thankful for his parents. This made a world of difference. I tried to keep the positive self-talk going so he wouldn't be so hard on himself and he would develop confidence so he could make the transition.

Chapter 14: What I Learned During Inpatient Admission and Resources Used

What I Learned During His Inpatient Admission

Since Mahalek was making huge improvements and the likelihood of him being able to go to public school was looking more promising, I wanted to make sure I was knowledgeable about things to prepare him for that transition. Those old feelings and concerns I had about the IEP resurfaced along with what else I needed to know to prepare him for public school. Although things worked well with the IEP developed by the school system he was enrolled in while at PHP, I needed the things addressed by PHP to be included in the IEP for public school. I didn't want Mahalek to go to a new school, have a meltdown, and the school not knowing the resources needed or have the goals in writing that needed to be addressed. My main concern was being an effective advocate for Mahalek during this time. My previous certification as an Autism Specialist had not been renewed for a few years. I let that certification expire during my rebuilding stages after the divorce. I decided to look into getting it renewed and learned about an updated certification that included more than just autism. In the program I learned about the specifics of autism, attention deficit hyperactivity disorder (ADHD), dyslexia, reinforcement strategies, universal design for learning (UDL) strategies, 504 plans and the IEP. I was very interested in learning more about cognitive disorders, not only because of Mahalek, but also in my position as a nurse educator. I had just taken a course of UDL strategies and ways to be more inclusive of other learning styles and disabilities, so I felt like this program was a good fit. This led to me getting my certification as Board Certified Cognitive Specialist. It helped me in determining next steps for Mahalek, including developing materials he may need, and assisting him with his academics.

    My support system was essential during this time. I had a hard time previously accepting the fact that my support system looked different than what I envisioned. Sometimes I would be so hard on myself or depressed at the fact that I didn't receive support from those that I thought would want to support me. I let those feelings subside and leaned on the support that I had at that time. My support was more in the sense of professionals or those I networked with. The nurses that I worked with in the past were able to give me anticipatory guidance on what to expect during Mahalek's admission and who were familiar with the providers employed there. Mahalek's therapists at PHP often checked in on me and supported me, not only during his admission as an inpatient, but while at PHP as well. They did quite a bit of work looking up and reaching out to others for resources that were helpful to me. I had someone at my job direct me to a state program to apply for a respite care voucher I qualified for to help lighten some of the financial burden. I had a few close friends that I spoke with often to express how I felt, especially during Mahalek's admission. There was someone who was there in every way imaginable to make sure I was supported and reassured me that my decisions were correct. I'm very thankful for the support that I had and feel blessed that I was able to stay in a positive place.

I learned how to be open to different perspectives and develop resources to help with Mahalek's compliance. It was recommended to develop a system to help him learn how to be consistent in his behaviors and what that meant. Mahalek was often inconsistent and worked hard to get an incentive, then once he got it, he didn't put in as much effort to regulate as he should. I started with using a calendar white board to track his good days. He was working on having fourteen good days in a row that would count toward the beginning of his consistency. At the end of the two-week period, he could either earn a privilege back that was taken away or get an incentive. The difference with this resource was Mahalek managed it. He used dry erase markers to track his days. If he had a tough day during that two-week period, those two weeks would reset. We marked his two-week mark with magnets. After he made it to two weeks, to try to keep him on track, there were random days with gifts or drawings of certain things he could earn. I learned that Mahalek was very triggered by electronic devices such as his Amazon Kindle tablet. I knew he would get fixated and sometimes had a difficult time transitioning off of it. For example, when he had a rough day, I took away his tablet and he had the opportunity to earn it back in two weeks. I noticed how he improved during that time. He found more ways to engage in creative play and was more compliant with the rules.

However, the minute he made it to two weeks and earned his tablet back within twenty-four hours he became more defiant and irritable. It took a few cycles of going through this pattern for me to notice the trend. Now it's a rare occurrence that he has his tablet to encourage those positive behaviors.

What Resources I Used During His Inpatient Admission

I embraced focusing on my work while he was admitted as an inpatient and his last few levels at PHP. I know working needs to be cut off at a certain point to maintain a good balance. My position as an administrative nurse educator was to oversee the nursing and allied health academic curriculums. This was an ongoing role that extended beyond the typical 9:00 a.m. to 5:00 p.m. schedule. I began to be more mindful of the balance and was more efficient at work during Mahalek's admission because I could focus without thinking about having to leave suddenly. I began to work on tasks and to get ahead on some things so I could stay balanced when he returned home. When I made it home, I shifted gears and focused on other things that were not related to work to stay in a balanced mental state. This helped me renew my passion for educating others and being a nurse. At times my motivation to continue with my career was stifled a bit by my feelings of it interfering with my ability to be a parent. I realized during Mahalek's admission that I should be able to function in my career effectively and maintain my motivation while being a parent. This is when I really was committed to setting realistic goals and boundaries with Mahalek after discharge. He needed to understand what his expectations were and how his behaviors cannot interfere with what I needed to do to provide for us.

I continued to touch base with a counselor that I used in the past regarding Mahalek's progress. The counselor was able to help guide me with ways to get important points across to Mahalek and help him put his behavior into perspective. Counseling helped reveal some of the sadness and hurts Mahalek was dealing with on top of the changes with everything. Therapy made me more mindful of expressing my emotions to him, so he understood he was not alone, and that I had feelings too. I remember him telling me he thought I was perfect and didn't have any sad or angry feelings. When I allowed him to see me work through those feelings in a positive light, it helped him learn I was human like him. This really helped open our relationship. We were able to work through feelings at home to prevent some of the intense emotions that would have led to a meltdown.

Once Mahalek was discharged from his inpatient stay, I included a set daily workout time and regimen for him. We started working out together for at least thirty minutes a day in the evening. To keep Mahalek motivated, I let him pick the workout videos we did together. He struggled at first to stay on track, for the first three weeks, until he got used to working out. Then I noticed he had issues with his balance, so I included yoga at least twice a week. This was familiar to him when he was an inpatient. They had the kids do yoga to keep their anxiety under control. I used this time between his flag football season to help get him in better shape and help ease his tension so he could regulate better. At first, he was not confident in his ability to work out and said it was too hard. I let him know that if he stuck with it, he would play better during flag football season, and that was a motivating factor for him. After a while he started to get excited at the fact that he could hold a pose in yoga better and his flexibility improved. There was a time his occupational therapist mentioned that he had a weak core which affected his ability to concentrate on his schoolwork. This was discussed in the IEP meeting toward the end of the school year when he was in the third grade. I let her know, as well as the team, that Mahalek had started doing yoga at home so hopefully that would improve his core sooner than later. Mahalek was a very active child anyway and started to develop a passion for working out. Sometimes Mahalek went with me on short runs. I began to have him engage in some sort of physical activity to help calm him down when he was irritated. We would do the activity until he was able to ask me questions or discuss his feelings. He started to look forward to doing some sort of physical activity and sometimes included his stuffed animals.

Chapter 15: Transition to Public School

Mahalek's transition to public school was no small task. I'm no stranger to juggling multiple things at once, especially when it comes to his services, but quickly found myself feeling overloaded. Mahalek's transition to public school for the fourth grade began the summer before. The summer was so full with contacting multiple people to get him set up with the things we knew he needed and what was recommended. PHP began the transition with slowly tapering off his days. He ended up only going four days a week instead of five, since I was off on Fridays, to see how he would handle the adjustment. It was always understood and communicated that if Mahalek had a hard time transitioning, he would just resume full time at PHP until he was ready. When PHP proposed cutting his days down to four instead of five, I knew I had to find him a place to attend on Fridays so he wouldn't get used to staying at home with me. He still had some trouble with separation anxiety and I didn't want to set him back with unrealistic expectations as he transitioned. Also, I wanted to see how Mahalek would handle a change to a different environment with peers around his age. I thought it would be a good time to test and see if he could use his coping strategies appropriately.

I began to look for summer camps or programs he could attend on Fridays that were appropriate for children with autism. I found a newly established sensory gym that was like the one Mahalek attended before and was located close to my job. I went in to see if they had any openings. They only had an opening for a few weeks toward the end of summer which didn't really fit into the transition plan. However, I went ahead and reserved that time just in case I couldn't find anything else. The search for a place Mahalek could attend increased my anxiety at the time. I found myself reflecting on our experiences before he began at PHP. I was afraid that he wouldn't be able to handle the environment and I would be stuck without childcare.

I thought of the time I had placed Mahalek at a home daycare close to our home as we were waiting on his start date at PHP. Mahalek had attended the daycare for a few days and did well. I thought it might have been a good fit since the daycare provider and her husband were nurses and seemed so receptive to Mahaleks' needs. Then one day, they played music, and everyone started dancing and Mahalek got beside himself and attempted to run out of the house. I was immediately called to pick him up. When I stated it would take me at least thirty to forty-five minutes to get there and I was on my way, the frustration I picked up on was so disappointing. After I got off the phone, I called around to see if there was anyone I knew that was close enough and willing to pick him up until I arrived in the area. I found someone who ended up picking him up ten minutes before I got into the area. During that time it took for him to be picked up, I received several calls asking if someone could come quicker, with underlying tones of frustration and anger, based on his multiple attempts to leave the house. After I picked up Mahalek and talked with him about the situation, about ten minutes later I got a call from the provider that Mahalek was not welcome back based on his behavior and that the money I paid for the week would be refunded. Mahalek never returned and I never did receive a refund. After Mahalek's dismissal from the home daycare, I had a conversation with my employer to see if I could work virtually for a few weeks until he transitioned into PHP.

These past experiences made me nervous about placing him somewhere, even if it was a short time, over the summer. However, I knew that my job would work with me if I needed to stay home with him for a short while as I was looking for a placement. I just didn't want to delay his progress. After a week of expressing my concerns and searching around for placement, I spoke with a friend who recommended a local camp where Mahalek would have a friend there and see a familiar face. It took me a few weeks to come to terms with trying the summer camp at the Christian school. I went to sign him up for Fridays which were field trip days. Once I found the placement, I let PHP know and we began tapering his days. To prepare Mahalek for the days at the summer camp, I sat with him, and we made a transition guide. I wanted to test it out to see how effective it would be before he started. Mahalek needed something to reference to keep him on track. We put together a guide with pictures he selected, along with coping strategies, contact information, and pictures he could use if he started to miss home since that was sometimes his reasoning for having a meltdown. I attached a guide to his lunch bag so he could reference it throughout the day with snacks and lunch. He did well for the first few weeks.

One day he had a tough time during the drop off time at the summer camp and I was unsure if he could pull it together. I had mixed up my times and went to drop him off at the summer camp when the other children had already left to go to the museum. Mahalek was so sad and upset that he wasn't on the bus. He was looking forward to riding with them on the bus. I was told I could take him there myself and he could ride the bus back so that's what I did. During the whole car ride Mahalek and I discussed how he felt. I tried to redirect him about missing the bus and accepting that I had the times wrong, but he could still attend for the day. Mahalek was having a hard time so I let him have some time to see if he could calm himself down. After we arrived at the museum, he was still upset, but wanted to go inside. I let him know if he couldn't calm down and stay calm, I had to bring him back with me and he would miss the trip for the day. He wanted to try and as he went in and one of the teachers greeted him with a few of the kids he immediately calmed down and was ready to participate. Overall, that ended up being a good day for him.

When he attended summer camp, I made sure I stayed close to the school in case there were any problems. The next week Mahalek went with the children to one of his favorite indoor entertainment centers. He was so excited to go and ride the bus. Riding the school bus ended up being the highlight of his day. I had a quick work meeting close to lunch hour that day and then I received a call from the school that I needed to get to the center as soon as possible because Mahalek was having a meltdown. I quickly left and headed in that direction. I was delayed due to a car accident and had to take an alternate route. Although I was telling the school how far away I was and keeping them updated, I still received multiple calls about where I was and why I hadn't arrived. When I got there one of the teachers gave me an update that he was upset because he wanted more money on his card, she told him no despite others getting extra money on their game cards, and he lost it.

At this time Mahalek was calm and sitting with the bus driver. After I got him in the car and he was calm enough for him to tell me his side of the story, there was a simple fix on the school camp's side that could have avoided the entire situation if they were properly trained in how to deal with autistic children. Mahalek had run out of money on his game card, and had they let me know I could have provided more money. Instead, they didn't validate his concerns and proceeded with adding money to the other children's cards. Mahalek didn't think it was fair. I didn't support or excuse Mahalek's behaviors at all and he accepted his consequences. However, it was additional confirmation that if I wasn't careful about placing him, I would keep running into the same issues. This made me feel like my options were so limited. Later that day, I received the call that I anticipated. Mahalek could no longer attend the camp since they were not equipped to deal with him when had a meltdown. I was back to square one.

Since it was close to the start of school, I was able to take some time off to keep him at home and PHP worked with my schedule up until that start to help with childcare. PHP wanted me to express my concerns with his upcoming transition to public school. At that time, my biggest concern was having before and after school care appropriate to what Mahalek needed. They looked around for additional places while also researching ABA services that had openings. I realized the public school he was transitioning into had a program there, but I was unable to contact someone since it was still summer months. I ended up visiting the school district's administrative offices to see if there was anyone who could let me know if the school still had openings for the before and after school programs. I had left a few messages for the Directors in the district. Then I found an email address and started sending an email to the principal to ask about openings for the before and after school programs. I explained my reasoning for requesting him to be placed at the school to keep him in a consistent environment if possible. After a few weeks, I received a reply that my information would be passed along to see if there were still spots open and I would be notified prior to the start of school. In the meantime, I went ahead and completed all the necessary paperwork to get him enrolled in the district. I placed him on a few waitlists of after school programs within the area as possible backup options.

As I was searching for a before and after school program and completing the enrollment process, I was also following up with finding another ABA placement as recommended by PHP. Mahalek's therapist at PHP contacted a behavioral therapist in the area who contacted people she knew to see if there were any places with openings. PHP researched ABA services that were supported by evidence that they felt would be appropriate for Mahalek. There were several I called that either were full or placed me on the waitlist and didn't follow up with me. PHP recommended outside ABA services to be an additional support for me as Mahalek transitioned into public school. After searching for a month there was one ABA company that had openings and was willing to get Mahalek started. However, they didn't inform me of what the possible schedule looked like until Mahalek started school. They wanted to split time and have Mahalek attend ABA in either the morning or afternoon and then school at the opposite time. I had been in communication with the district's principal all summer of the possibility and waiting on approval services with his school schedule. I didn't receive a response stating their thoughts until Mahalek started in public school and had a meltdown. However, based on my lack of assistance with getting Mahalek to and from services I decided not to start him at the ABA therapy center, based on the distance and time it would take me to commute to each place daily, and my inability to take daily extended lunch breaks at work. I communicated this with the school and ABA company. I continued to look for ABA providers that could provide in-person services after school. Meanwhile, the school had ABA therapists employed within the district come by occasionally to observe Mahalek.

Around this time Mahalek started attending a social skills class, arranged with a local non-profit organization with pre-teens, at a local therapy center. I signed him up to begin the class as the summer started. I wanted him to become more confident in interacting with peers, outside of PHP, to ease his anxiety and fears about bullying. Mahalek was under the impression that the things he saw as an inpatient and at PHP would be like public school. Despite my attempts to tell him it's a more relaxed and different experience, I wanted him to hear it from a peer perspective. Mahalek still needed to work on appropriate interaction with peers and responding within the context of the conversation. Sometimes he had issues with sarcasm and didn't realize his peers were joking with him. Other times he was so literal and fixed on specific details it made it difficult for him to understand the true context of the conversation. Social skills class ended up being a huge success that enhanced his ability to interact with his peers and he made a few friends along the way.

In the process of these moving pieces, I was in constant communication with the school principal to get him set up for school. I sent his current IEP and requested a meeting to update it as he was transitioning along with feedback from PHP. PHP helped with the process. They collaborated with all group members to develop a handout to compile quick tips to get to know Mahalek. The quick tips included what his triggers were, his likes and dislikes, and what helped him stay calm with coping strategies that helped during his time there. This was eventually passed along to the teachers in public school during the back-to-school night. The principal was very responsive during this time and was informing the team about my requests to update his IEP and all other materials I provided. I was worried that if his IEP wasn't updated, to address his behaviors with his upcoming discharge from PHP, that I would have limited ability to protect him in the public school setting. To help put things into perspective, I provided a list of Mahalek's latest incidents from PHP that was a part of the intake process for ABA therapy. I wanted the school to be aware of what could potentially happen if there was no preparation for the transition. I tried my best to keep them in the loop and cover all bases. PHP was honest with me in the process of things and let me know that it would be a process at first and I needed to be patient with them and Mahalek as they taught each other.

Chapter 16: What I Learned About the Transition and Resources Used

What did I learn as he transitioned to public school?
I learned we both had anxiety about the transition. Mahalek was concerned about bullies and I was concerned about how the teachers would respond to his needs. As much as I tried to comfort Mahalek, I had to practice coping strategies alongside him to maintain my composure. The positive self-talk was something we both engaged in on a regular basis while we were in the car. I had to show him that I was confident in my abilities to get everything in line for him to make a successful transition. To be honest, it was going to be a transition for both of us. I learned that my anxiety was a result of the past experiences he had in other places and my ability to be present if I was needed or called. I didn't have the best support when it came to someone stepping in at the school or program over the years when there was a problem. I did my best to try to prepare for that. Luckily at work, I was able to explain my situation to my supervisors and they were very understanding, supporting me in whatever I needed to do.

This eased my anxiety a bit knowing I had the flexibility with my job. I learned how to navigate around Mahalek's unpredictable schedule and plan at work to stay on task as I addressed what I needed to for him.

I learned Mahalek was more ready for the transition than I thought. Mahalek's communication of his feelings had significantly improved. For instance, I remember him saying he was excited to make new friends at his new school and eat in the cafeteria. I took him to his cousin's back-to-school night a few days before his was scheduled so he could see how she handled everything. He had a stuffed animal with him to comfort him and was very open about his feelings of being nervous in a new environment. He realized that his cousin was just as nervous too, about going to a new grade with a new teacher, and she was able to cope just fine. When his back-to-school night came he was nervous. However, that quickly disappeared when he interacted with his homeroom teacher. She engaged him and had him put away his school supplies that were included in his bag. He found his desk and followed the instructions that were asked of him. He began to become excited about this new journey. We went for a small tour and discussed before and after school care. I honestly thought he would have a problem with before and after school care, so I started with after school care initially to transition him. Come to find out, on day one, he loved after school care. I learned he was eager to make it through the day just to have some time with friends during their after-school care program that was structured and fit his needs.

I learned ABA may need to be revisited. As he transitioned to school, I was still working on the placement in ABA that would work best for him. When I realized that the ABA company I had been in contact with wanted to split the days for him to go to therapy half the day and school half the day, I had to explore other options due to my inability to drop him off and pick him up in multiple locations throughout the workday. When Mahalek started public school, he expressed how much he liked interacting with his classmates. I had discussed with him the opportunity for him to go to ABA therapy, which may require him to leave school early or come later. He immediately expressed that he did not want to do that, because he wanted to be with his friends, and he wanted to be treated the same as the other children. I learned that he wanted social interaction and the interruptions in his school schedule would exacerbate his behaviors, so I looked for other ABA options.

What Resources I Used to Help Him Transition to Public School

I provided a one-page handout, the school transition guide, and a weighted belt to help Mahalek and the teachers with his transition. These were a few things I passed along to the school to help them as Mahalek started. The ones I mentioned previously were the "Getting to Know Mahalek" handout that PHP had created, and the school transition guide I piloted at the summer camp. Prior to this first day of school, Mahalek and I updated the school transition guide to include his class schedule, math charts, and reading sight words to help with his schoolwork. The teachers expressed their gratitude for the resources to help them with Mahalek as they were learning his behaviors. Mahalek was so eager to get started and stay as calm as possible he became more open to using whatever resources were necessary. To supplement the handout and transition guide, we made weighted belts from old weights we had lying around from a weighted vest that no longer fit him. The weight belt was used across his lap and neck, while completing schoolwork, to help with focus and anxiety. Sometimes he just kept it in his backpack, but the weight of the backpack kept him at ease. We discussed how these resources should be used during our short walk to class every day. I learned Mahalek was open to finding ways to cope with his anxiety and go to public school like the other kids.

I started to read more to help stay mentally and emotionally balanced throughout the process. I became a fan of self-help and spiritual books over the past few years. They helped me stay positive along my healing journey. With Mahalek transitioning into school, I started to incorporate reading back into my nightly routine. These books helped me slow down my thoughts and stay grounded in the present to stay level headed enough to support Mahalek through his transition. One book that I slowly worked through was about cognitive behavioral therapy. It included exercises I could slowly work on throughout the week to process my feelings. After I did a few of these exercises, I read some of my spiritual books to keep me grounded in my faith. As Mahalek worked through his feelings I was in a place to help him with understanding the new routine at school and conversations he was having with his peers. The books were a form of therapy and I used some of the techniques I learned with Mahalek to help him process his feelings.

I learned how to keep consistent communication with the school using written documentation. I was used to documenting and keeping records in my role at work. However, with his transition to school I followed up with things in writing to hold them accountable and validate my efforts collaborating with them. The school was very responsive and open to this communication. I was very transparent with communication in person as well but wanted to have them reference information in writing depending on what steps needed to be taken next. Mahalek had so many people working together to provide him with a great education so written communication to all parties kept us all on the same page. Sometimes, I would follow up with written communication after he had tough days and I processed through it so I could respond appropriately. I learned how to communicate additional strategies that may be helpful for Mahalek to address behaviors noted by the school so everyone could reference it. I wanted them to understand that I was an active parent who was willing to do what was necessary to make sure Mahalek was in a safe environment and help minimize his unsafe behaviors.

Chapter 17: Present Time

Mahalek's transition to school has been a learning experience. The first month he was in class his teachers and staff were receptive to his needs and helped him work through the day. Within a few weeks, there was an incident that I was notified of because Mahalek was asked to join the special education class for math and reading. He became defiant and aggressive because he wanted to stay with the rest of the regular education class. He had pulled it together that day, but I had a hard time the next day. That next day he had a meltdown. This incident was the first one at the school in which the resource officers had to be called. Mahalek was so upset he ran out of the classroom and went back to his homeroom kicking the door and starting to hit the staff. He was placed in a hold and removed from the area. When I arrived, he was in a calm state and in a classroom with two resource officers. As the staff and principal filled me in, I was trying to process my feelings of my child acting out and not able to give my thoughts for next steps. It took me a while to process the incident and I typically responded with my feedback in writing within forty-eight hours after the incident. The resource officers were great. However, I still couldn't get over the fact that the older he got, the more at risk he was of dealing with officers in a way I was afraid of. I had a hard time understanding how this incident came about because I wasn't notified of him needing to change to a different classroom. Then I remembered how PHP told me I would need to be patient with everyone.

After each incident Mahalek had at the school, we started the next day and week fresh. The staff at the school was great at reinforcing the fact that the next day was a new beginning. As school started to get more demanding for Mahalek, in terms of schoolwork, he began to have more difficult days. I was concerned that he would be in a situation where I couldn't advocate for him because my attempts at having an IEP meeting had not been followed up on at the time and we were about six weeks into the school year. Mahalek was in a few holds monthly that resulted in the school either calling me to let me know or sending restraint documentation to me via email. There were several days that he was in a soft hold just to help him calm down and refocus. The school tried their best and I gave them as much information and assistance as I could in the process. However, my patience was wearing a bit thin waiting on a follow up response about his IEP and management of his behaviors.

One day I dropped Mahalek off at school and noticed the school staff seemed to avoid me and went into a separate classroom. I just happened to be walking to the office to pay his fee for before and after school care. I thought that was odd. It was the beginning of the week after Mahalek had had an incident the prior week. I had planned on speaking to the teacher that morning after I made his payment to discuss what plans they had for the Mahalek. I wanted to see if I needed to rearrange my schedule to be close in case he was resistant to going to the special education classroom. When I looped back around his teacher was surprised to see me, but quickly filled me in. The one thing she mentioned was she just got out of a meeting regarding Mahalek to determine the next steps. I wasn't sure how I felt about that because I was under the impression I should have been included in that meeting. Part of the reason Mahalek had a hard time that day was because they failed to transition him appropriately, so they decided to remove the transition to the special education classroom. I informed him that I should be included in changes in his schedule, so I could help him adjust as well, to help minimize his meltdowns. After that communication with them they started to loop me in a bit more.

I met with a special education teacher to get more insight on suggestions for developing appropriate goals for Mahalek to include in the IEP and to make sure he has appropriate accommodations. After the meeting with her, I drafted an email with my suggestions and sent them to the school for review. After a few weeks, I got a reply from the school to schedule the IEP meeting that I requested. Along with scheduling the meeting, I attended a conference regarding special education laws to learn more about how to advocate for Mahalek during the IEP meeting. I attended the conference for about thirty minutes before I got a call from the school that Mahalek had a meltdown and needed to be picked up. I was instantly in a mental fog and just packed my things up to get him.

A lady at one of the booths had approached me about the services they were advertising and I just expressed to her that I had to leave to pick up my son. As I walked out of the building that lady flagged me down and started to ask me a few questions about my situation because she wanted to help. She gave me her contact information and recommended me to come back with Mahalek. When I got to the school, I was so frustrated with Mahalek. I ended up pulling myself together and bringing him back to the conference. While we were on a break some of the special education teachers and counselors interacted with Mahalek and mentioned that some of his issues in school may be attributed to a learning disability, whether his abilities were below average or above average. I connected with a counselor who ended up being my parent advocate at the IEP meeting and offered to complete a learning disability screening and evaluation for Mahalek to help determine how to address his academic needs.

During his IEP meeting, the parent advocate and I determined that the school did not do any testing or was not addressing his academic needs. Mahalek's behaviors had been such a barrier to his academics that it was easy to overlook his struggles. Mahalek had the tendency to refuse to do his schoolwork even if he could complete it. This made it very difficult for anyone to screen him appropriately and get an accurate assessment of where he was academically. I notified the school of the plan to get him screened for learning disabilities and schedule an updated psychological re-evaluation. The school ended up using the initial psychological evaluation, and not the updated one given when generating his IEP. I had to resend the information and bring it up during the meeting to get it corrected. After the IEP meeting, I started the process of getting him screened for learning disabilities and scheduling his two-year psychological evaluation.

The process of completing Mahalek's learning disability screeners was a different experience. For instance, I realized that this was something that had to be completed outside of the psychological evaluation. Throughout Mahalek's clinical observations with the therapist it was determined that the school needed additional resources to help them de-escalate Mahalek and help him with coping strategies. I had already developed an incentive chart, that was updated with incentives Mahalek could earn based on good behaviors, the use of coping strategies for use at home and a one-page handout for the substitute teachers he had that week. The one-page handout listed coping strategies and de-escalation techniques that have been effective for Mahalek and one he identified himself. When I discussed this with Mahalek's therapist, who was completing the learning screeners, she suggested I send the sheet she created as well and include her in the emails to help expedite things to loop in outside assistance. I did as she suggested and then received a call from the special education director regarding my emails and requests. She was very responsive. We agreed that Mahalek needed a comprehensive evaluation completed by the school, since one was never done, and it would be arranged as soon as possible. The therapist and parent advocate ended up becoming my support to alleviate some of the burden of helping him transition to public school.

Despite the ongoing struggles and pending evaluations scheduled for Mahalek, he has made a huge improvement. The more he matures the more he begins to understand the consequences of his actions. He only becomes clouded during his meltdowns which lately have led to a few suspensions. I have been very concerned about the suspensions. I'm working hard to help him with his behavior to prevent any legal or safety issues. I really do not want Mahalek to have a criminal record, nor do I want to be in a position where I must deal with anything legally on his behalf. The scary part is he is growing up fast so he's getting bigger and stronger every day. The bigger he gets, the more destruction he causes, and the more he is seen as a threat. I will do everything in my power to protect him, within reason, and get him the resources he needs. I am blessed to not only have a strong spiritual base, but someone in my corner who has been my number one supporter. He knows who he is. I wouldn't have stayed as level and progressed this far with Mahalek if it wasn't for him. I know there will be more obstacles to overcome and the journey will be messy. However, I'm remaining hopeful that Mahalek will continue to improve and grow into a productive individual. I want people to understand they are not alone in their struggles with special needs children. At least that is what I want. To feel supported, understood, and heard throughout the process so I can remain strong as I raise this beautiful human into the man he is intended to be.

Acknowledgements

I would like to thank Allah, God, for giving me the strength to endure all that I've been through. My faith is what has kept me going and sane. Some days I look back and often wonder how I got to the place I am currently. I'm grateful to have developed a strong spiritual faith and Allah has kept me on the right path. I'm thankful Allah has blessed me to become a mother.

Thanks to my son, who is referred to as Mahalek, for loving me unconditionally and trusting me to be his safe place. I've learned how to be a better person and mother because of him. His patience with me along my healing journey has been instrumental in my progress. His understanding that his mother is not perfect has helped ease my tensions when it comes to raising him. He is truly a happy and loving son. I'm very grateful to be his mother.

Thanks to the therapists who helped Mahalek get to this point. Overcoming those mental health stigmas that are cultivated in our community has been a freeing experience for both of us. Your patience, honesty, and hope that we will improve for the better is appreciated. Therapy has been a rocky road, for both of us, that we are continuing to pursue. However, it has allowed us both to learn how to express our emotions properly and strengthen our relationship.

Lastly, thanks to my love, who has supported me every step of the way. He has listened to me and remained present throughout my healing journey without judgment. I've learned the true meaning of full support, acceptance, and unconditional love in a way I never thought I would experience. His strength has motivated me to keep going. His belief in me as a woman and a mother has inspired me to dream bigger and step out of my comfort zone. It is hard to put into words how appreciative and grateful I am to have such a beautiful soul in my life. I'm grateful for you pushing me to become greater and put into motion something that I did not think was possible.

www.ingramcontent.com/pod-product-compliance
Lightning Source LLC
LaVergne TN
LVHW011420080426
835512LV00005B/178